Note for Librarians: a cataloguing record for this book that includes Dewey Decimal Classification and US Library of Congress numbers is available from the Library and Archives of Canada. The complete cataloguing record can be obtained from their online database at:

www.collectionscanada.ca/amicus/index-e.html

ISBN 1-4120-4119-8

TRAFFORD

Offices in Canada, USA, Ireland, UK and Spain

This book was published *on-demand* in cooperation with Trafford Publishing. On-demand publishing is a unique process and service of making a book available for retail sale to the public taking advantage of on-demand manufacturing and Internet marketing. On-demand publishing includes promotions, retail sales, manufacturing, order fulfilment, accounting and collecting royalties on behalf of the author.

Book sales for North America and international:

Trafford Publishing, 6E–2333 Government St.,

Victoria, BC v8t 4p4 CANADA

phone 250 383 6864 (toll-free 1 888 232 4444)

fax 250 383 6804; email to orders@trafford.com

Book sales in Europe:

Trafford Publishing (uk) Ltd., Enterprise House, Wistaston Road Business Centre, Wistaston Road, Crewe, Cheshire cw2 7rp UNITED KINGDOM

phone 01270 251 396 (local rate 0845 230 9601)

facsimile 01270 254 983; orders.uk@trafford.com

Order online at:

www.trafford.com/robots/04-1926.html

10 9 8 7 6 5 4 3 2

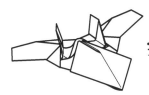

Interlocking and 3D Paper Airplanes

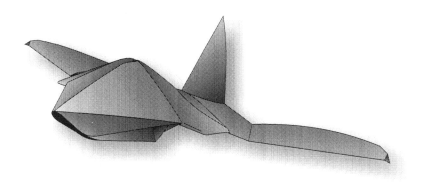

Teong Hin Tan

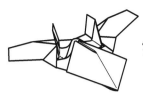

Special Thanks

To my wife, Lily, for her encouragement and proofreading, which made this book possible.

To my son, Kevin, for getting me interested in paper airplane folding in the first place, as well as the fun we shared in folding and flying paper airplanes.

To my daughter, Natalie, for her support in my writing this book.

To my sister, Phaik Luan, for test folding and her valuable suggestions regarding the folding steps.

For my parents, Gie Bie and Siew Kuan.

Contents

Introduction

Many people, young and old, are familiar with folding and flying paper airplanes. Paper airplane folding is truly wonderful, and full of fun because it is a hands-on activity, where you get to create the airplane yourself. The material cost is next to nothing. The time taken is short. You can put your imagination to work, and be creative with your paper airplane designs. Finally, you get to test fly them, and see how well they fly. Later on, while trying to figure out a way to get your paper airplane to do a certain maneuver, you may even learn a thing or two about the science of aerodynamics and flight controls. It is something that you can do all by yourself, or with your family and friends.

As an engineer in the aviation industry, my paper airplane designs tend to be heavily influenced by my desire for better aerodynamics, structure and performance. In that effort, I have created what I call the "Interlocking Paper Airplane" in order to meet those requirements. This book contains instructions to fold sixteen of my favorite inter-locking and 3D paper airplanes.

The designs and folding concepts are all originals, and they are probably amongst the most sophisticated and beautiful paper airplanes you have ever seen.

Each of these interlocking paper airplanes is made from just an ordinary sheet of 8.5" x 11" paper without any cutting or gluing. Using the unique interlocking fold, wing fold and fuselage fold, you will be amazed at how an ordinary sheet of paper can be transformed into a tightly bound paper airplane, with beautiful and seemingly impossible three dimensional fuselage. These airplanes are also great fliers because of their streamlined fuselage, which blend in smoothly with their well-structured wings. It may be hard to imagine, but 3D paper airplanes, despite their larger fuselage, actually have very little drag for their size because of their streamlined shapes.

The unique interlocking fold is the key to the interlocking paper airplane's ability to hold its own shape tightly together, resulting in superior structure, aerodynamics and performance. Whether you are a

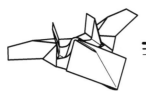

frequent paper airplane folder or someone new to paper airplane folding, it is very likely that you will find great joy in folding and flying interlocking and 3D paper airplanes.

It is also very likely that you may find yourself folding and flying nothing else, but interlocking and 3D paper airplanes from now on.

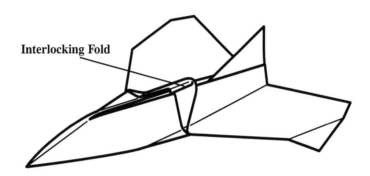

Interlocking Fold

Special Interlocking Fold holds the fuselage tightly together

Airplane Features

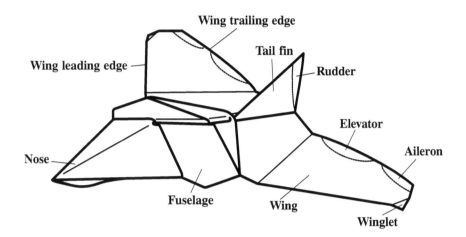

Main features of a 3D paper airplane

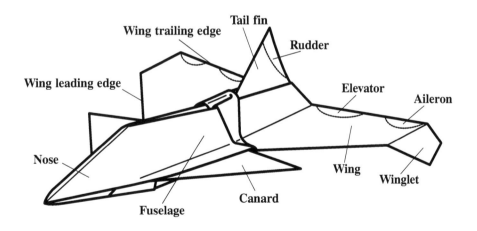

Main features of a canard paper airplane

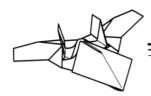

Symbols

Model outline

Crease line

Hidden line

·······················

Valley fold

- - - - - - - - - - - -

Mountain fold

-·-·-·-·-·-·-·-·-·-·-

Push in the arrow direction

Turn model over

Fold in the arrow direction

Unfold

Fold and unfold

Fold behind or fold under

Fold according to number sequence

1   2   3

Marked point

o

Destination point

×

Dimension line

Equal distance lines

Basic Theory

FORCE BALANCING

Unlike conventional airplanes, paper airplanes are essentially gliders because they do not have engines to propel them forward in a horizontal flight. Paper airplane depends on its weight, thanks to gravity, to keep it moving in a downward sloping path. All together, there are three forces, weight, lift and drag, acting on a paper airplane in flight.

Once a paper airplane is launched with a forward thrust from your fingers, it moves forward, and gravity exerts its influence to pull the airplane earthward at the same time. The resulting air current, moving over its wings, generates an upward lifting force called lift, which is perpendicular to the flight path, to counteract the opposite weight component of the airplane. Lift helps to keep the airplane aloft. The same air current, moving over the airplane, also generates drag, which acts in the opposite direction of the flight path, due to air resistance. Drag slows the airplane down; however, during the gliding phase of the flight, the weight component, parallel to the downward sloping path, counteracts drag to keep the

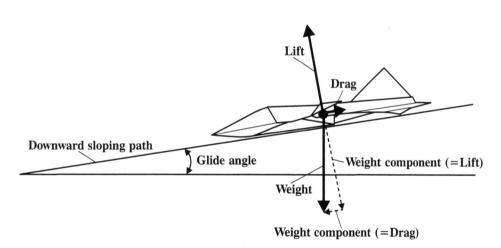

Forces acting on a paper airplane in steady glide

airplane moving forward. With all three forces at balance, the paper airplane trades altitude for speed as it moves along the downward sloping path until it hits the ground, or something else in its path. The angle of the downward sloping path is equal to the lift/drag ratio, hence the more lift and less drag an airplane has, the smaller will the angle of the downward sloping path be, and the further will the airplane glide for a given amount of altitude loss.

For the initial phase of flight, immediately after launching, the airplane seems more as if it is flying instead of gliding. In fact, it can actually maintain level flight for a certain distance or even gain altitude. Why is this the case if paper airplanes are supposed to behave like gliders? The answer is, at the point of launch, you impart a certain amount of energy to the airplane. The harder the throw, the more energy is imparted. The airplane leaves your fingers at a higher speed than it would normally require to glide on its own. The higher speed and energy level allow the airplane to generate extra lift to maintain

level flight or to climb. This energy will eventually be used up to counteract drag, resulting from air resistance, and to attain a higher altitude if the airplane climbs. The airplane will slow down to a point where it begin to glide, and start trading altitude for speed.

Where does lift come from? Paper airplane wings, although more layered towards the leading edge than the trailing edge, are still relatively flat when compared to the airfoil-shaped wings on conventional airplanes. Nevertheless, the same aerodynamic principles still apply where lift generation is concerned. As air approaches the wing's leading edge, at a small angle of attack, it divides at a point called the stagnation point, which is a little below the front of the wing's leading edge. The air going over the top of the wing then progresses forward around the leading edge, where it separates from the wing because it is unable to adhere to the surface around the sharp edge. However, it is turned backward by the main flow, and reattaches to the upper surface a short distance from the leading edge.

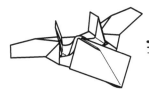
The overall non-symmetrical flow pattern around the wing causes the air to get sucked down, and to accelerate over the top surface of the wing, so that it exits the trailing edge in a streamlined manner. The end result is that the air above the wing travels at a faster speed than the air below the wing. The faster moving air, above the wing, produces a lower air pressure than the slower moving air below. The difference in air pressure across the wing then produces a net upward force called lift, which keeps the airplane aloft.

The greater the angle of attack, the greater is the amount of lift and drag being generated. However, there is a limit, which is not very much, and typically less than 10 degrees, where linear lift generation is possible. Beyond this limit, the air will suddenly separate from the upper wing surface completely and cause the wing to stall. When the wing stalls, total lift will be lost and the airplane crashes.

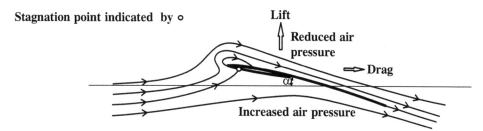

Paper airplane wing at small angle of attack, α, and generating lift

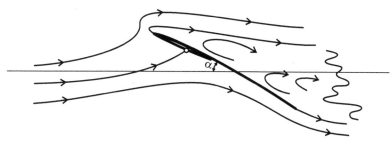

Paper airplane wing at large angle of attack, α, and flow separation

STABILITY

A paper airplane is capable of proper flight only if it is stable both statically and dynamically. A stable airplane in flight is one which, when disturbed, will automatically bring itself back to its original course. A stable airplane must, therefore, have longitudinal, directional and lateral stability. Longitudinal stability refers to an airplane pitching its nose up or down. Directional stability refers to an airplane yawing to the right or left, and lateral stability refers to an airplane rolling clockwise or anti-clockwise. Careful design and selection of the airplane's fuselage, wings, fins, vertical and horizontal stabilizers, as well as the location of the center of gravity, are necessary to ensure stability.

Without getting into the complex theory regarding airplane stability, the following are generally true of a paper airplane, and may be useful to help you understand and make a better, or a more stable, paper airplane on your own:

➤ Moving the center of gravity towards the front of the airplane will enhance longitudinal stability. The same is also true for having a smaller wing area towards the front, and a larger wing area towards the rear of the airplane.

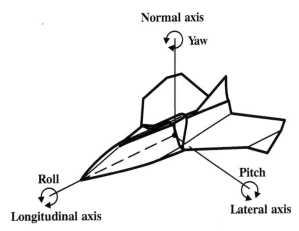

Three axes of a paper airplane

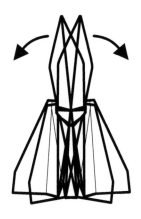

Yaw Movement

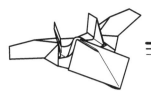

➤ Having more vertical surface such as fuselage, fins, wingtips and tail fin behind the center of gravity will enhance directional stability.

➤ Having sweptback wings, dihedral wings or positioning the center of gravity below the main wings, will enhance lateral stability.

Too much of anything is not necessarily good, and the same is also true for airplane stability. An airplane with too much longitudinal stability will nose dive to the ground in front of you. An airplane with too much directional stability, and not enough lateral stability, can cause "Spiral Divergent" in which the airplane suddenly rolls to one side and spiral-dive to the ground. An airplane with too much lateral

stability, and not enough directional stability, can cause "Dutch Roll" in which the airplane continues to yaw to one side, rolls back, yaws to the other side and rolls back again. The trick to a stable airplane is to make sure that the airplane has just the right balance of stability in all three directions.

All the paper airplane designs in this book have basically the right balance of stability built in, but that still does not mean that they will fly well upon completion of the fold. You would still need to learn to trim an airplane in order to make the airplane fly the way you want it to fly. Trimming in this case means adjusting the control surfaces, and this is being addressed in another chapter called "Trimming Instructions".

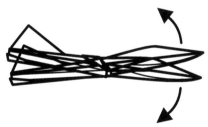

Pitch Movement

Roll Movement

Folding Instructions

Used photocopy, printer and writing papers, measuring 8.5" by 11", are perhaps the most easily available types of paper, and they are all great for paper airplane folding. The entire fleet of paper airplanes in this book has been designed based on this paper dimension. My personal preference is for the heavier gage paper because of its stiffness, which makes for a stronger crease and therefore a stronger paper airplane. However, any paper, measuring 8.5" by 11", that has been used or unwanted would be just as suitable.

To make a good paper airplane, it is crucial that each and every fold is made as accurately as possible, and every matching fold as symmetrical as possible. Matching fold refers to folds that are mirror image of each other. This is especially true at the beginning as each misalignment in the fold gets amplified and compounded by the next fold. A paper airplane with misaligned and mismatched folds will most likely not fly very well. For a start, it is recommended that you follow the suggested dimensions in the book until you are familiar

with the folds, and could make changes as required to achieve the desired result.

The importance in making every crease sharp, after each fold, is just as crucial. Creasing the fold properly, after each folding step, will help to ensure the accuracy of the fold that follow. Sharp and matching crease, on the fuselage and wing, has a great impact on the aerodynamics and performance of the paper airplane. You will notice that as more folds are added, the paper gets thicker. With added thickness, some of the earlier creases may become a little out of place. That is the reason why it is always a good idea to re-crease and flatten all folds, after each step, in order to reestablish their crease lines.

Many people like to use their thumbnails to crease paper folds. Creasing with thumbnails will not only produce less consistent result, it can also be painful and damaging to your nails if you happen to fold a lot of paper airplanes like I do. My recommendation is to use an unwanted plastic card. Expired

telephone cards and hotel key cards are examples of plastic card you can use to sharpen paper creases, as well as to flatten out paper folds over a large area.

Get familiar with the symbols used and their meanings. Before you make a fold, always study the diagrams carefully first. In this book, the current diagram shows both the results from the previous fold, and the current fold instruction to get to the next diagram. Study both current diagram, as well as the next diagram, in order to get a better understanding of how the current fold should be made.

The fleet of paper airplanes in this book is arranged in the order of increasing difficulty. It is suggested that you start from the beginning. As you progress through each model, you will become more familiar and experienced with making the folds. By the time you get to the more difficult models, they may not be all that difficult after all.

There are three particular folds that I thought might be a little more challenging. They are shown in the "Practice Folds" chapter so you can refer to them for more details when required. The "Practice Folds" is actually a good place to start, even if you are already familiar with paper airplane folding. You can practice and sharpen your folding skill here before moving on to folding the actual paper airplanes.

Trimming Instructions

The trailing edge of a paper airplane's wings and canards can be used to act as elevators to provide pitch control for nose up or nose down adjustments. The outer trailing edge portion of the main wing can be and proper trimming of the airplane. An airplane can be trimmed to fly fast, slow, straight or curve. The first few throws are executed to find out how the airplane actually flies so corrections can be made to get the

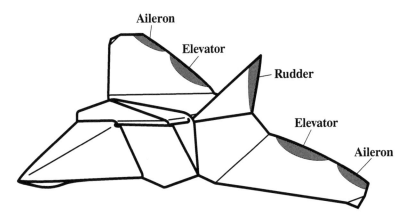

Control surfaces on a typical paper airplane

used to act as ailerons to provide lateral control for roll adjustments. The trailing edge of the vertical tail fin and winglets can be used to act as rudders to provide directional control for turning right or turning left.

The success of a flight depends on good airplane symmetry

airplane to fly the way you want it to.

Before anything else, the first thing to do is to check for proper airplane symmetry. Make sure that both wings are balanced, and that they are attached to the fuselage at the same dihedral angle. Check that the tail fin is straight and vertical, and winglets are balanced.

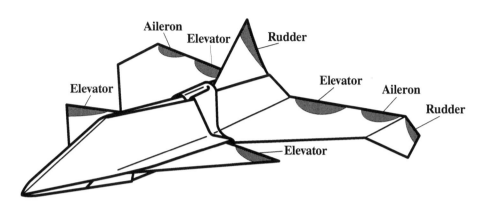

Control surfaces on a canard airplane

The best way to trim an airplane is by pinching the trim surface between your thumb and index finger, and then pulling your pinched fingers away and at the same time bending the trim surface towards the desired trim direction. Repeat the action several times, and bending only a little at a time. A little trim can sometimes have a great effect on the flight, and several trial flights and trimmings are usually required in order to get the airplane to fly properly. Gently toss the airplane during trial flights, and work your speed up once the airplane is properly trimmed.

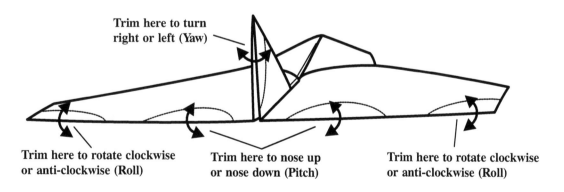

Moving direction of the elevators, ailerons and rudder

The following are some of the more common problems that can be expected during test flights, and what you can do to correct them:

► **Airplane pitches down and hits the ground.**
- The airplane is longitudinally too stable, and this is a very common phenomenon with most paper airplanes. Correct by bending the elevator up. However, for a fast throw, the amount of up elevator trim required will be less than that for a slow throw. For an airplane with canard, the elevator on the canard should be bent downward, while the elevator on the main wing upward.

► **Airplane pitches up, stops and then crashes to the ground.**
- The airplane has stalled because it is longitudinally unstable. Correct by bending the elevator down. For an airplane with canard, the elevator on the canard should be bent upward, while the elevator on the main wing downward.

► **Airplane curves gently to the right or left.**
- Correct by bending the trailing edge of the tail fin or winglets towards the direction you want the airplane to go. For example, to curve more to the left, bend the rudder towards the left.

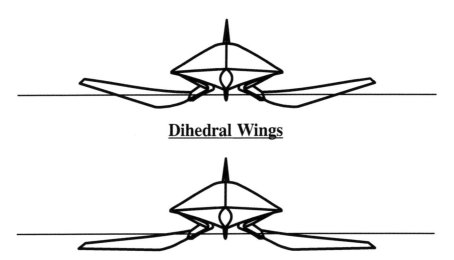

Dihedral Wings

Anhedral Wings

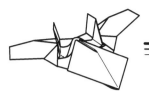

➤ **Airplane goes into a roll or spins around the longitudinal axis.**
- The left and right wings may not be balanced. Check for proper symmetry of the airplane. Looking from the rear of the airplane, a clockwise roll tendency can be corrected by bending the right aileron down and the left aileron up, and vice versa for an anti-clockwise roll tendency.

➤ **Airplane flies for a short distance, and then flips around and crashes.**
- The airplane is directionally unstable. Correct by increasing the size of the tail fin or adding winglets.

➤ **Airplane curves sharply to one side, and spiral dives to the ground.**
- This is a sign of the airplane having a "Spiral Divergent" problem. The airplane has too much directional stability and too little lateral stability.

Correct by adding more wing dihedral, or reducing the size of the tail fin.

➤ **Airplane rolls from side to side, and wagging its tail.**
- This is a sign of the airplane having a "Dutch Roll" problem. The airplane has too much lateral stability and too little directional stability. Correct by reducing the wing dihedral, increasing the size of the tail fin and/or adding winglets.

➤ **Airplane is totally out of control. It flips around and drops right in front of your feet.**
- The center of gravity could be too far back, making the airplane unstable. Correct by reducing the wing's size in the front and increasing the wing's size at the back. Add or shift some weight towards the nose.

Flying Instructions

The proper way to launch a paper airplane is by holding its "keel", on the underside of the airplane, between your thumb and index finger or between your thumb, index and middle fingers. The entire fleet of paper airplanes in this book is designed with a "keel" for launching

and then glide gently down for the rest of the flight if it didn't hit anything along the way.

For stunt action, add lots of up elevator for over the head loop or sideways loop. For sideways loop, throw the airplane at an angle.

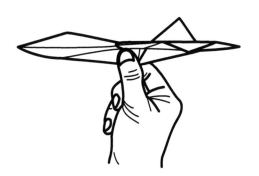

Holding with thumb and
index finger

Holding with thumb, index
and middle fingers

purposes. Pull your arm back and then swing fast-forward, flip your pinched fingers forward and then release the airplane straight forward. After release, follow through with a smooth arm movement.

A properly trimmed airplane should fly straight or with a slight curve. It may gain some altitude after launch, reach the top of climb,

For fast and straight flights, reduce the amount of pitch by trimming the elevator down, and then throw the airplane hard, and vice versa for slow flights.

Since the only way a paper airplane is going to land is by crashing onto something or hitting the ground, it is very likely that it will sustain some sort of deformation

or damage upon each "landing". You will need to check the airplane, before each flight, to make sure that you have corrected any misalignment or damage from its previous, eventful, "landing".

A useful trick you can do in order to get your 3D interlocking airplanes to fly even faster and farther, as well as to provide more stability for flights under windy conditions, is to add weight to the hollow interior of the fuselage. I have done this by stuffing shredded pieces of tissue paper into the hollow fuselage cavity, and then taping the opening shut to prevent the tissue paper from falling out. The external shape and contour of the 3D paper airplane will remain more or less the same, but the now heavier airplane will be able to fly faster, and more stable under windy conditions. Just remember that you will need to add more up elevator in order to counter-act the added weight in the front of the airplane. Bon Voyage!

Practice Folds

All the paper airplane models in this book are made up of pretty much the same few types of fold. Three of the more challenging folds are shown here, in order to provide more diagrams, to help you better understand how they are made. The three folds are:

➤ Inside Reverse Fold
➤ Wing Fold
➤ Interlocking Fold

The "Inside Reverse Fold" is particularly useful for introducing a step towards the front portion of the airplane's fuselage and wings. It enables the creation of another wing section in between the nose and the main wings for a more impressive fuselage look.

The "Wing Fold" is one of the most useful folds, and more than 80% of the airplane models in this book use the wing fold. Wing fold allows the construction of wings that contain a hollow section along the underside of the wing's leading edge. The hollow section functions as wing spar to provide structural support for a stiff wing. In addition, the hollow section also helps to maintain a slight camber, resembling that of an airfoil, at the front of the wing, for a more superior aerodynamics. Lastly, the wing fold allows the construction of wings that wrap around the fuselage, at the point where they both meet, resulting in a more streamlined joint.

The "Interlocking Fold" is by far the most important and useful fold. Without it, the entire fleet of paper airplanes in this book will not be called interlocking paper airplane. The interlocking fold locks the two halves of the paper airplane tightly together, allowing the construction of 3D fuselage as well as some very streamlined airplanes. It is the main contributor to the interlocking paper airplane's superior structure, aerodynamics and performance.

Take your time to become familiar with these three folds before you start on the actual paper airplane models. Once you have mastered these three folds, you are well on the way to become an expert in folding interlocking and 3D paper airplanes.

1. Inside Reverse Fold

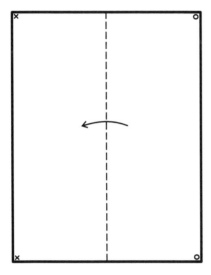

1. Fold the paper in half.

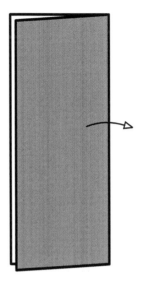

2. Unfold to its previous position.

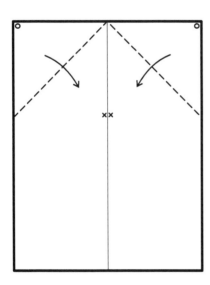

3. Fold the marked corners to the center crease line.

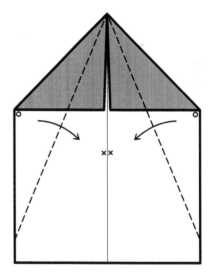

4. Fold the marked corners to the center crease line.

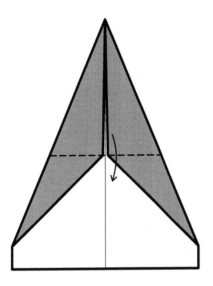

5. Fold the tip down the center crease line along the fold line as shown (see "Tip" on page 22).

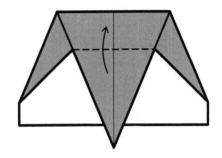

6. Fold the tip up the center crease line along the fold line as shown (see "Tip" on page 22).

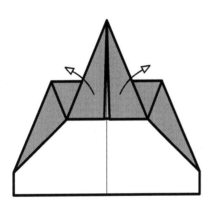

7. Unfold model to step 4 position.

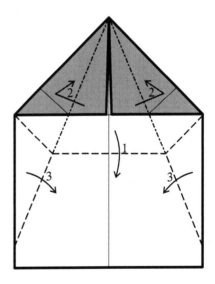

8. Make an inside reverse fold by following the fold lines' numbering sequence.

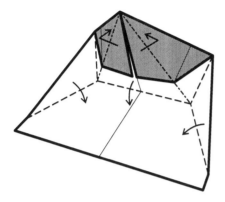

9. Model shows the intermediate stage of the fold from step 8 to step 10.

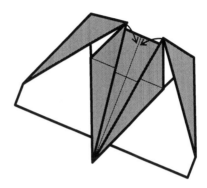

10. Fold down corners and crease the edges.

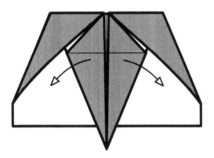

11. Unfold the top layer.

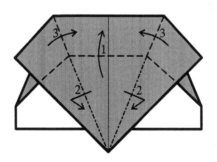

12. Make another inside reverse fold by following the fold lines' numbering sequence.

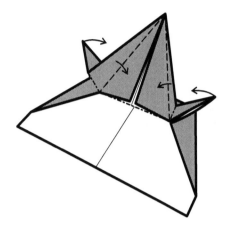

13. Model shows the intermediate stage of the fold from step 12 to step 14.

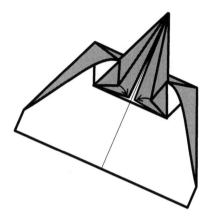

14. Fold down corners and crease the edges.

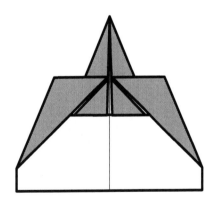

15. Completed "Inside Reverse Fold".

Tip: The more flexible the crease lines created in steps 5 and 6 are, the easier it is to make the inside reverse fold. To make the crease line more flexible, bend and crease the fold line once, in both directions, before moving on to step 7.

2. Wing Fold

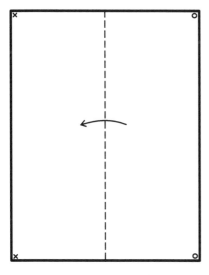

1. Fold the paper in half.

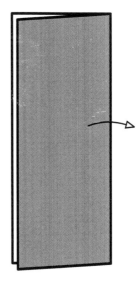

2. Unfold to its previous position.

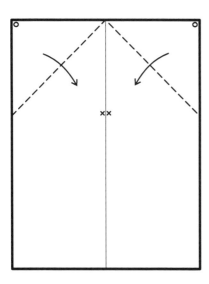

3. Fold the marked corners to the center crease line.

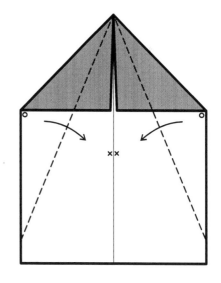

4. Fold the marked corners to the center crease line.

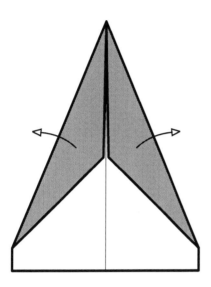

5. Unfold to step 4 position.

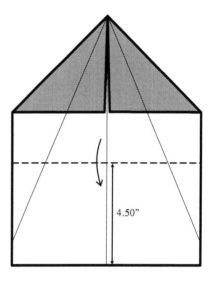

4.50"

6. Fold the tip down the center crease line.

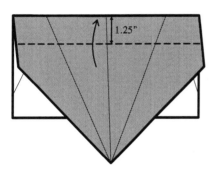

1.25"

7. Fold the tip up the center crease line.

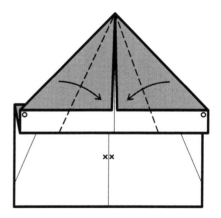

8. Fold the marked corners to the center crease line. More detail explanation in step 9.

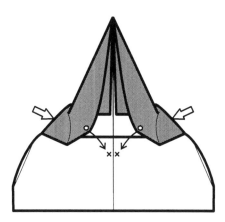

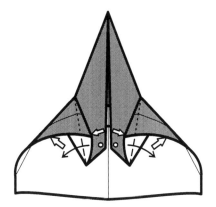

9. Push the two overlapping side folds inward as the two marked corners are moving towards the center crease line.

10. Hold the marked center part of the folds down. Push the lower portion of the two overlapping folds out, and valley fold. See next diagram for more details.

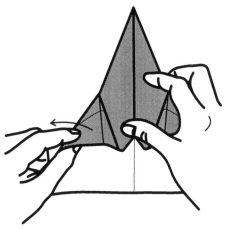

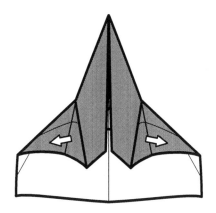

11. This diagram shows how the overlapping flap is folded outward.

12. Stretch the two overlapping flaps out, and then crease and flatten folds.

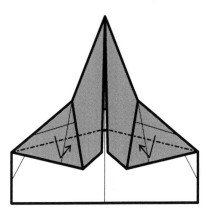

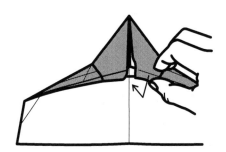

13. Fold the flaps under, and insert beneath the horizontal edge created in step 7. See next diagram.

14. Diagram shows how the flaps are folded under the horizontal edge.

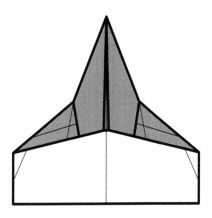

15. Completed "Wing Fold".

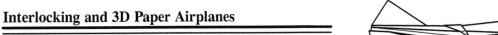

3. Interlocking Fold

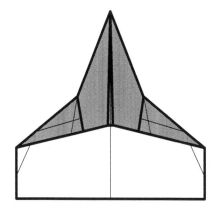

1. Start with step 15 of the completed "Wing fold" as shown above.

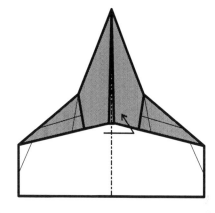

2. Mountain fold the model in half.

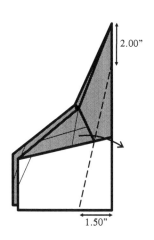

2.00"

1.50"

3. Valley fold the top layer of the model to the right side. This fold will result in the nose twisting upward a little.

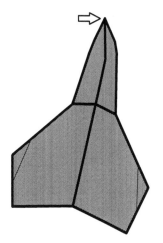

4. Gently flip the nose over to the other side. Do not let go of the model.

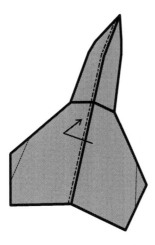

5. Mountain fold the left wing to match the right wing.

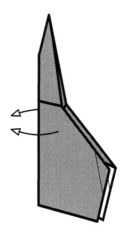

6. Crease the fold hard, and unfold model such that the shaded side of the model is facing upward.

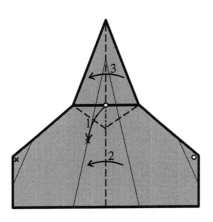

7. Using your thumb and index finger, lift the overlapping flap up. Valley fold such that the marked point, on the overlapping flap, meet the crease line marked with an 'x'. See next three diagrams for more details.

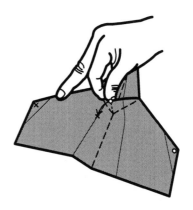

8. Model shows how the marked overlapping flap is being held between the thumb and index finger, with the thumb positioned under the flap.

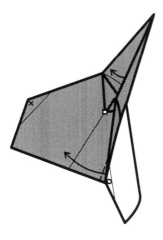

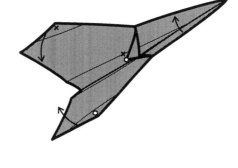

9. Hold the marked tip of the overlapping flap against the crease line as shown above. Make a matching fold on the right half of the overlapping flap. Continue to fold the right half of the model over to the left.

10. Model above shows the almost completed matching fold on the overlapping flap. Continue to fold the two halves of the model together.

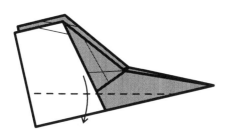

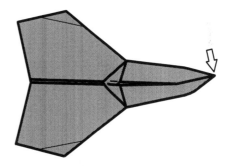

11. Valley fold the top layer of the model down along the existing crease line. This fold will result in the nose twisting upward a little. Be careful not to tear the interlocking fold on the inside.

12. Gently flip the nose over to the other side.

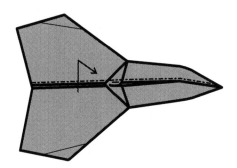

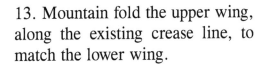

13. Mountain fold the upper wing, along the existing crease line, to match the lower wing.

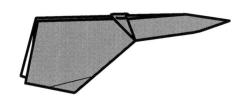

14. Completed "Interlocking Fold".

Note: The final position of the marked point, after steps 7, 8 and 9, will determine the quality of the Interlocking Fold. The goal is to get the marked point to line up exactly with the two crease lines, created in steps 3 and 5, when the two halves of the model come together in step 10. If the marked point position is below the crease lines, the result is a loose interlocking fold. If the marked point position is above the crease lines, the interlocking fold will tear when you fold both wings down in steps 11 and 13.

The Fleet

The fleet consists of sixteen of my favorite interlocking paper airplane models that I have developed over the years. Some of them have actually evolved from my earlier non-interlocking models.

Eight of the sixteen models have enclosed three dimensional fuselage, with a hollow cavity, similar to real airplanes. These models incorporate good streamlined body to ensure a lower drag. Structurally, they are amongst the strongest, but the best thing about them is their beauty. They are great as model airplanes, which you can place on your desk as decorations or as impressive giveaways. They are impressive mainly because most people have not seen, or even heard of, an enclosed three dimensional paper airplane folded from just a single sheet of paper.

The remaining eight models have fuselage of a different kind that offers an even lower drag. These high performance airplanes may not have enclosed fuselage, but their unique fuselage designs are just as impressive. For flying fun, they are my preferred choice.

I have had great satisfaction in creating these unique paper airplanes, and I have also had many hours of fun flying them. I hope that you, too, would find folding and flying interlocking and 3D paper airplanes to be just as much fun.

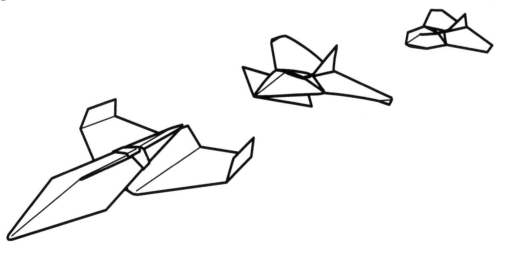

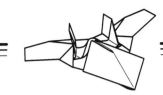

1. Cruise Missile

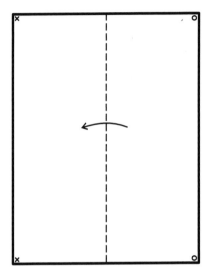

1. Fold the paper in half.

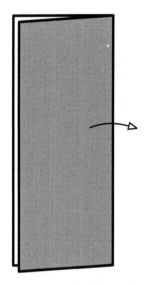

2. Unfold to its previous position.

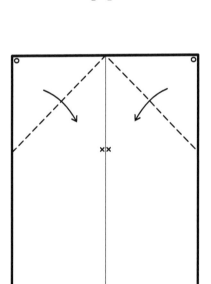

3. Fold the marked corners to the center crease line.

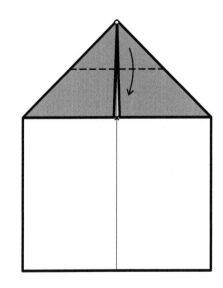

4. Fold the tip down the center crease line to the horizontal edge created in step 3.

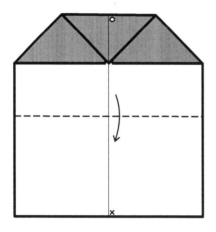

5. Fold the top horizontal edge down the center crease line to the bottom horizontal edge.

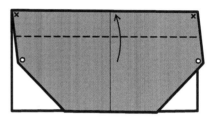

6. Fold the marked corners up to the top horizontal edge.

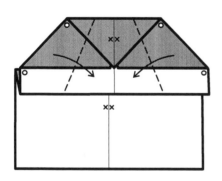

7. Fold the marked corners to the center crease line.

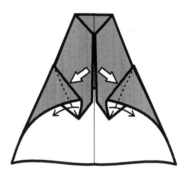

8. Hold the center part of the folds down. Push the lower portion of the two overlapping folds out, and valley fold (see "Wing Fold" on page 23).

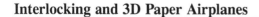

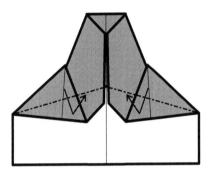

9. Fold the flaps under, and insert beneath the horizontal edge created in step 6.

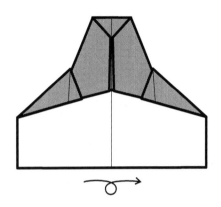

10. Turn model over.

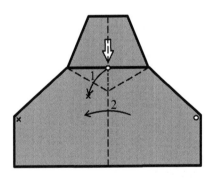

11. Lift the marked overlapping flap up towards you, and valley fold (see "Interlocking Fold" on page 27).

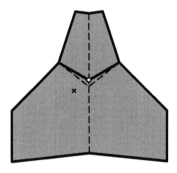

12. Model shows the intermediate stage of the fold from step 11 to step 13.

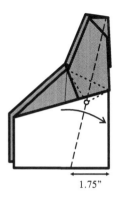

1.75"

13. Fold the top layer of the model to the right side. It is important to make sure that the fold line meet the marked tip on the hidden lines.

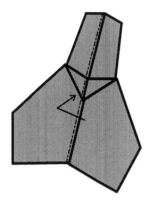

14. Mountain fold the left wing to match the right wing.

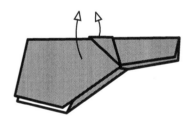

15. Unfold both wings to form a slight dihedral angle as shown in the completed "Cruise Missile" in the next step.

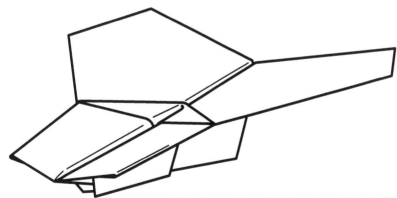

16. Completed "Cruise Missile".

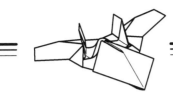
2. Falcon

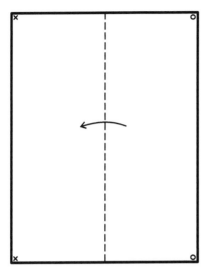

1. Fold the paper in half.

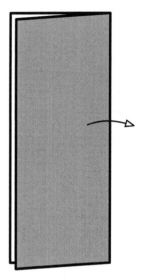

2. Unfold to its previous position.

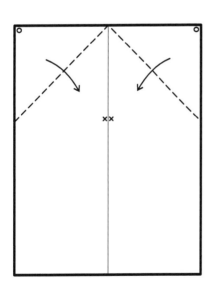

3. Fold the marked corners to the center crease line.

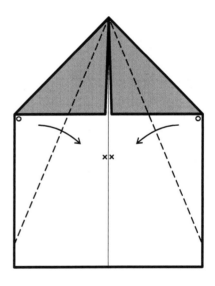

4. Fold the marked corners to the center crease line.

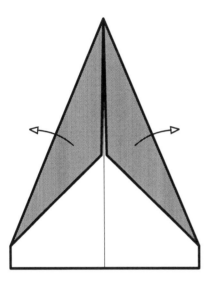

5. Unfold to step 4 position.

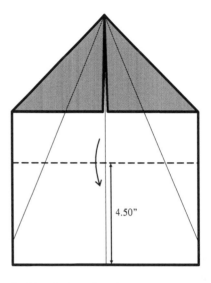

4.50"

6. Fold the tip down the center crease line at 4.50" from the bottom horizontal edge.

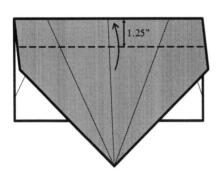

1.25"

7. Fold the tip up the center crease line at 1.25" from the top horizontal edge.

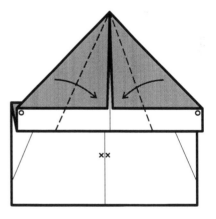

8. Fold the marked points to the center crease line.

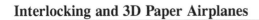

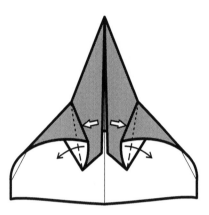

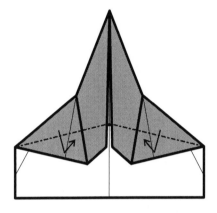

9. Hold the center part of the folds down. Push the lower portion of the two overlapping folds out, and valley fold (see "Wing Fold" on page 23).

10. Fold the flaps under, and insert beneath the horizontal edge created in step 7.

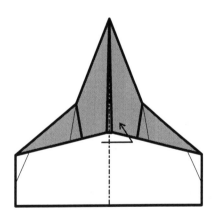

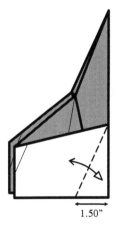

1.50"

11. Mountain fold the model in half.

12. Fold and unfold to create crease line for the tail fin.

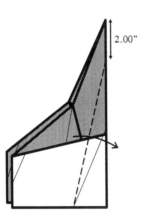

2.00"

13. Fold the top layer of the model to the right side. This fold will result in the nose twisting upward a little.

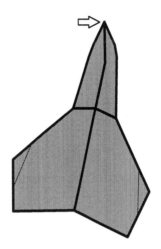

14. Gently flip the nose over to the other side. Do not let go of the model.

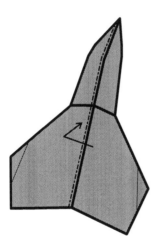

15. Mountain fold the left wing to match the right wing.

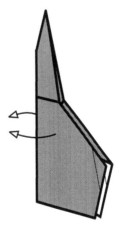

16. Unfold both wings.

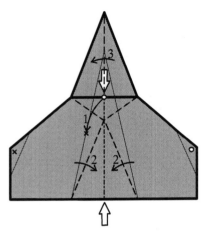

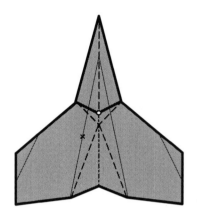

17. Lift the marked overlapping flap and the center of the bottom horizontal edge up towards you. Valley fold such that the marked point on the overlapping flap meet the crease line created in step 15 (see "Interlocking Fold" on page 27).

18. Model shows the intermediate stage of the fold from step 17 to step 19.

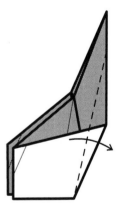

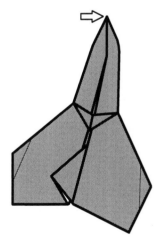

19. Fold the top layer of the wing to the right side along the existing crease line. This fold will result in the nose twisting upward a little.

20. Gently flip the nose over to the other side.

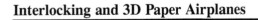

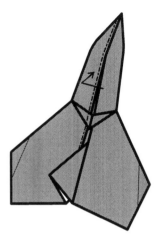

21. Mountain fold the left wing to match the right wing.

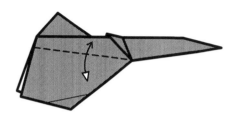

22. Fold and unfold both wings to create crease lines for wing dihedral. Turn model over to show bottom side.

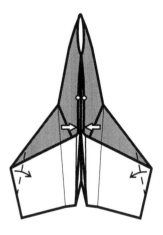

23. Pop open the fuselage by pulling out the marked paper edges. Holding the pulled out paper edges together with one hand, pinch down the excess paper bulge with the other hand at the location as shown by the two arrows. Crease wings' leading edge, and fold both wingtips along existing crease lines.

24. Model shows fuselage before step 23.

25. Model shows fuselage after step 23.

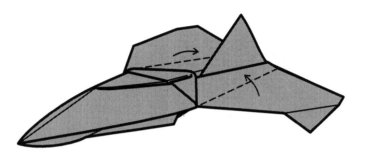

26. Bend both wings up a little, along the existing crease lines, for a slight wing dihedral.

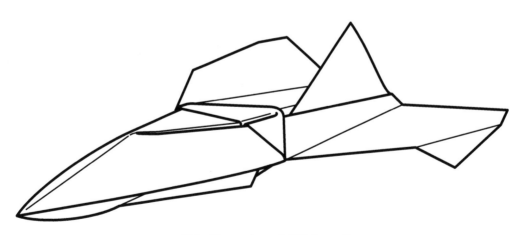

27. Completed "Falcon".

3. Mirage Fighter

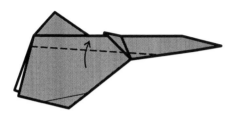

1. Make the above model by following step 1 through step 21 for the "Falcon". Fold both wings up to create the fuselage.

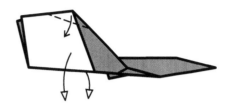

2. Unfold both wings to a level position. Crease wings' leading edge, and fold both wingtips along existing crease lines.

3. Adjust both wings to form a slight dihedral.

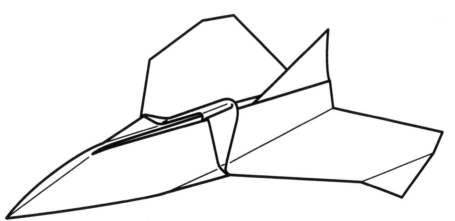

4. Completed "Mirage Fighter".

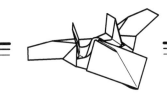

4. Cyclone

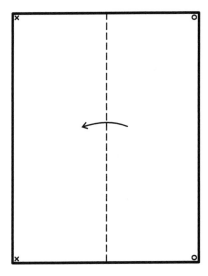

1. Fold the paper in half.

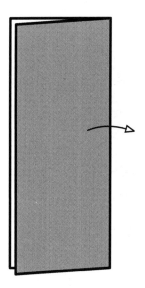

2. Unfold to its previous position.

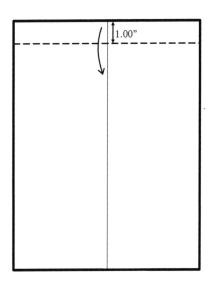

3. Fold the top horizontal edge down the center crease line at 1.00" from the top horizontal edge.

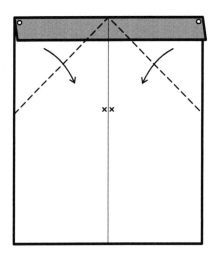

4. Fold the marked corners to the center crease line.

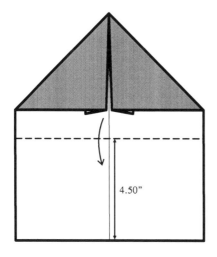

5. Fold the tip down the center crease line at 4.50" from the bottom horizontal edge.

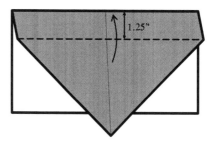

6. Fold the tip up the center crease line at 1.25" from the top horizontal edge.

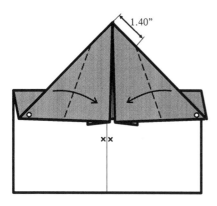

7. Fold the marked points to the center crease line.

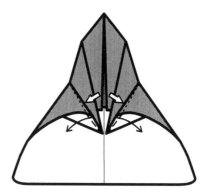

8. Hold the center part of the folds down. Push the lower portion of the two overlapping folds out, and valley fold (see "Wing Fold" on page 23).

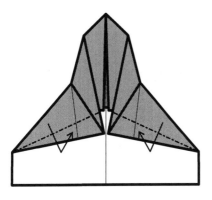

9. Fold flaps under, and insert beneath the horizontal edge created in step 6.

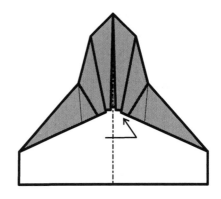

10. Mountain fold the model in half.

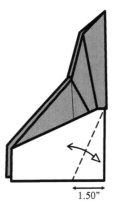

1.50"

11. Fold and unfold to create crease line for the tail fin.

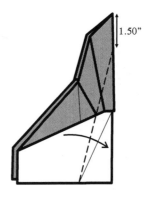

1.50"

12. Fold the top layer of the model to the right side. This fold will result in the nose twisting upward a little.

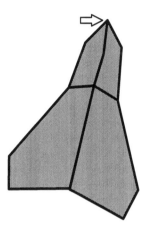

13. Gently flip the nose over to the other side. Do not let go of the model.

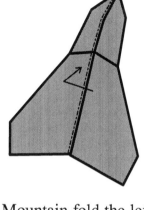

14. Mountain fold the left wing to match the right wing.

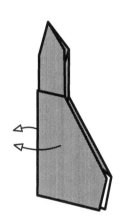

15. Unfold both wings.

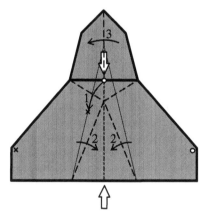

16. Lift the marked overlapping flap and the center of the bottom horizontal edge up towards you. Valley fold such that the marked point on the overlapping flap meet the crease line created in step 14 (see "Interlocking Fold" on page 27).

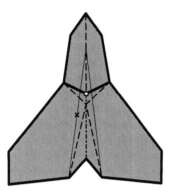

17. Model shows the intermediate stage of the fold from step 16 to step 18.

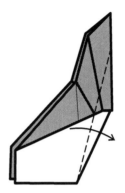

18. Fold the top layer of the wing to the right side along the existing crease line. This fold will result in the nose twisting upward a little.

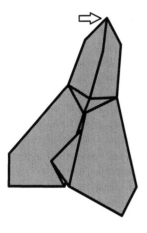

19. Gently flip the nose over to the other side.

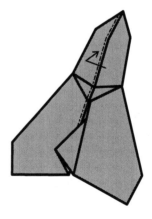

20. Mountain fold the left wing, along the existing crease line, to match the right wing.

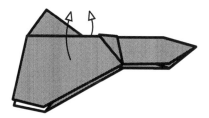

21. Open both wings, and turn model over to show the bottom side.

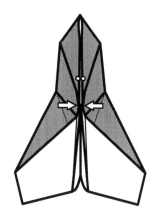

23. Model shows fuselage before step 22.

22. Pop open the fuselage by pulling out the marked paper edges. Holding the pulled out paper edges together with one hand, pinch down the excess paper bulge with the other hand at the location as shown by the two arrows. Crease wings' leading edge.

24. Model shows fuselage after step 22.

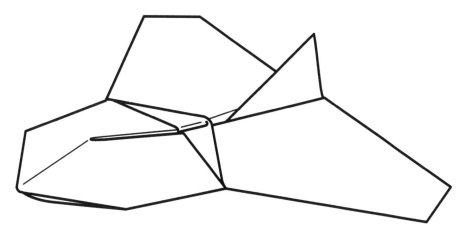

25. Completed "Cyclone".

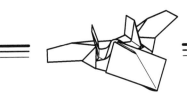

5. Sonic Rider

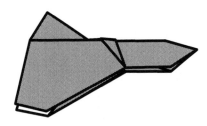

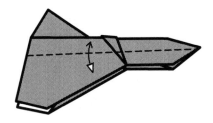

1. Make the above model by following step 1 through step 20 for the "Cyclone".

2. Fold both wings up to create the fuselage, and then unfold both wings down to a level position. Crease wings' leading edge.

3. Add a slight dihedral to the wings.

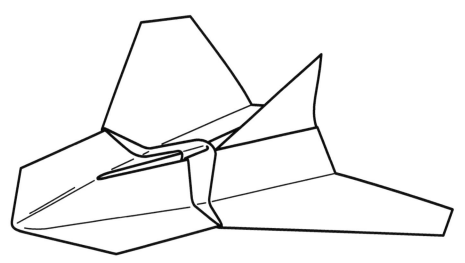

4. Completed "Sonic Rider".

6. Arrow Cruiser

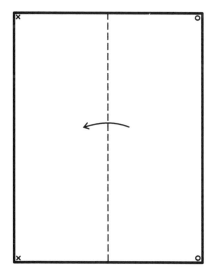

1. Fold the paper in half.

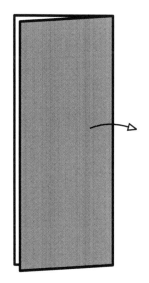

2. Unfold to its previous position.

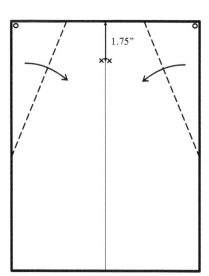

3. Fold the marked corners to the center crease line located at 1.75" from the top horizontal edge.

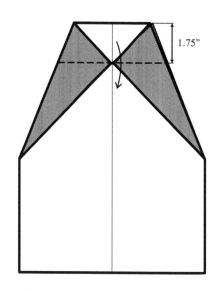

4. Fold the top horizontal edge down the center crease line at 1.75" from the top horizontal edge.

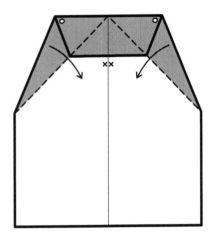

5. Fold the marked corners to the center crease line.

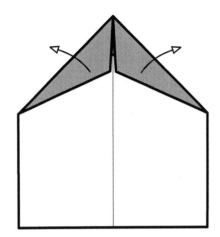

6. Unfold to step 4 position.

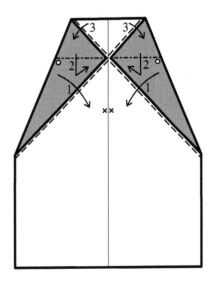

7. Fold the marked points to the center crease line to create a water bomb base.

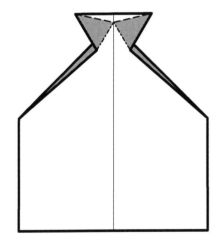

8. Model shows the intermediate stage of the fold from step 7 to step 9.

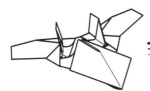

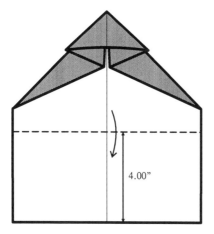

9. Fold the tip down the center crease line at 4.00" from the bottom horizontal edge.

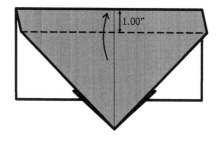

10. Fold the tip up the center crease line at 1.00" from the top horizontal edge.

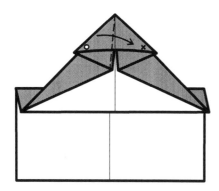

11. Flip the marked tip from the left to the right.

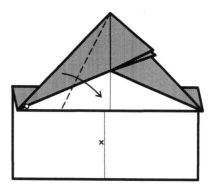

12. Fold the marked point to the center crease line.

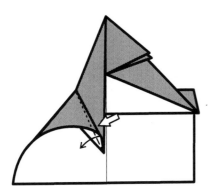

13. Hold the center part of the folds down. Push the lower portion of the overlapping fold out, and valley fold (see "Wing Fold" on page 23).

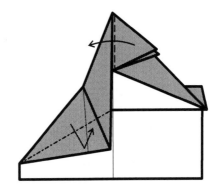

14. Fold the flap under, and insert beneath the horizontal edge created in step 10.

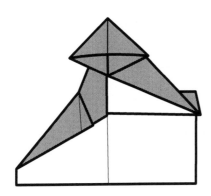

15. Repeat steps 11 through 14 for the right side.

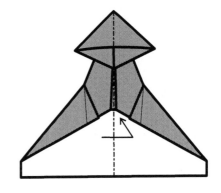

16. Mountain fold the model in half.

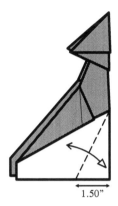

17. Fold and unfold to create crease line for the tail fin.

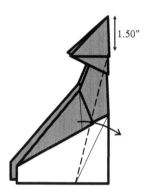

18. Fold the top layer of the model to the right side. This fold will result in the nose twisting upward a little.

19. Gently flip the nose over to the other side. Do not let go of the model.

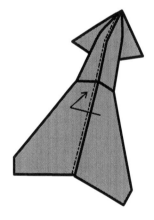

20. Mountain fold the left wing to match the right wing.

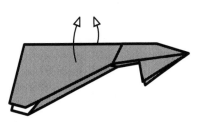

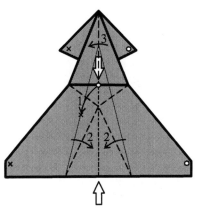

21. Unfold both wings.

22. Lift the marked overlapping flap and the center of the bottom horizontal edge up towards you. Valley fold such that the marked point on the overlapping flap meet the crease line created in step 20 (see "Interlocking Fold" on page 27).

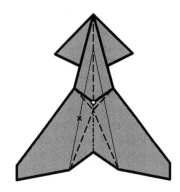

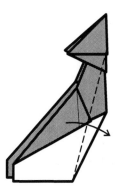

23. Model shows the intermediate stage of the fold from step 22 to step 24.

24. Fold the top layer of the wing to the right side along the existing crease line. This fold will result in the nose twisting upward a little.

25. Gently flip the nose over to the other side.

26. Mountain fold the left wing, along the existing crease line, to match the right wing.

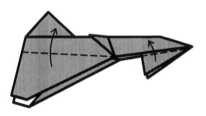

27. Fold wings and nose wings up to create the fuselage. Crease wings' leading edge.

28. Adjust the wings and nose wings to form a slight dihedral.

29. Completed "Arrow Cruiser".

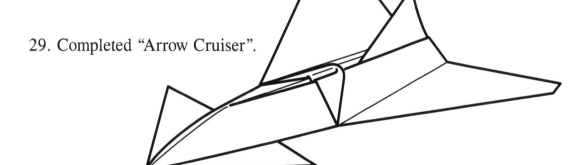

7. Fox Bat

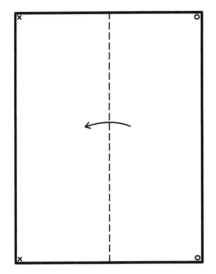

1. Fold the paper in half.

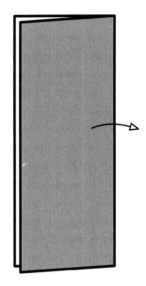

2. Unfold to its previous position.

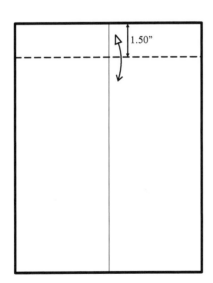

3. Fold and unfold the top horizontal edge down the center crease line at 1.50" from the top horizontal edge.

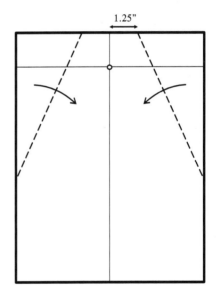

4. Fold both top corners down at 1.25" from the top center such that their top horizontal edges meet at the marked point.

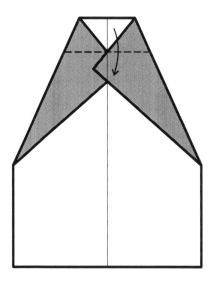

5. Fold the top horizontal edge down the center crease line.

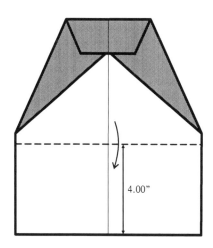

6. Fold the top horizontal edge down the center crease line at 4.00" from the bottom horizontal edge.

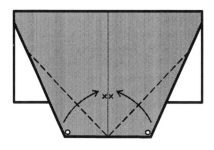

7. Fold the marked corners to the center crease line.

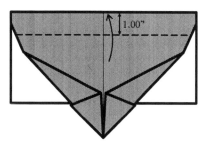

8. Fold the tip up the center crease line at 1.00" from the top horizontal edge.

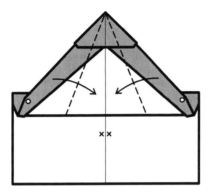

9. Fold the marked corners to the center crease line.

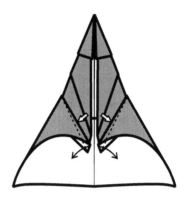

10. Hold the center part of the folds down. Push the lower portion of the two overlapping folds out, and valley fold (see "Wing Fold" on page 23).

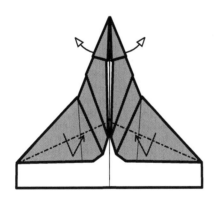

11. Fold both flaps under, and insert beneath the horizontal edge created in step 8. Flip open the two hidden triangular shaped nose wings from below the nose.

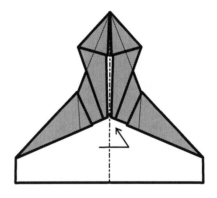

12. Mountain fold the model in half.

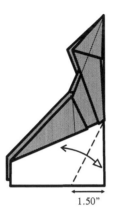

2.00"

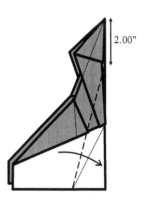

1.50"

13. Fold and unfold to create crease line for the tail fin.

14. Fold the top layer of the model to the right side. This fold will result in the nose twisting upward a little.

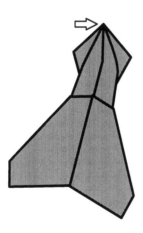

15. Gently flip the nose over to the other side. Do not let go of the model.

16. Mountain fold the left wing to match the right wing.

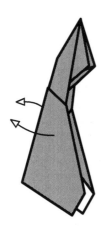

17. Unfold both wings.

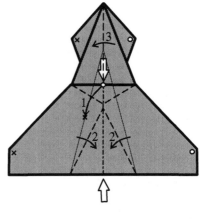

18. Lift the marked overlapping flap and the center of the bottom horizontal edge up towards you. Valley fold such that the marked point on the overlapping flap meet the crease line created in step 16 (see "Interlocking Fold" on page 27).

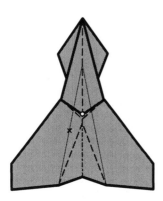

19. Model shows the intermediate stage of the fold from step 18 to step 20.

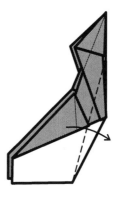

20. Fold the top layer of the wing to the right side along the existing crease line. This fold will result in the nose twisting upward a little.

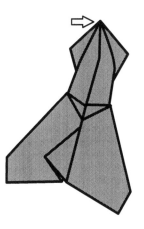

21. Gently flip the nose over to the other side.

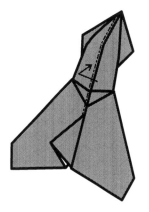

22. Mountain fold the left wing, along the existing crease line, to match the right wing.

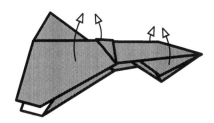

23. Unfold both wings and both triangular shaped nose wings a little.

24. Flip model over to show the bottom side.

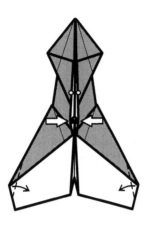

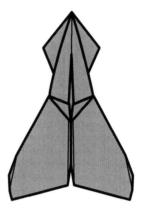

25. Pop open the fuselage by pulling out the marked paper edges. Holding the pulled out paper edges together with one hand, pinch down the excess paper bulge with the other hand at the location as shown by the two arrows. Crease wings' leading edge, and fold wingtips along existing crease lines.

26. Adjust the two triangular shaped nose wings such that they are horizontal and level.

27. Model shows popped open fuselage.

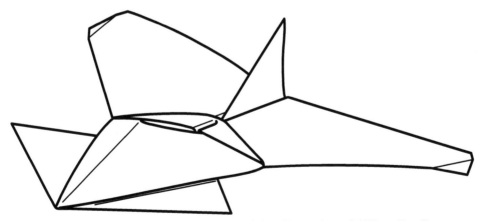

28. Completed "Fox Bat".

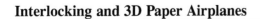

8. Diamond Cruiser

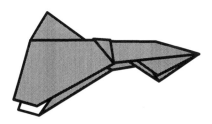

1. Make the above model by following step 1 through step 22 for the "Fox Bat".

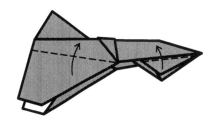

2. Fold both wings and triangular shaped nose wings up to create the fuselage.

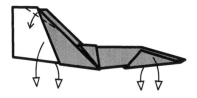

3. Unfold both wings and triangular shaped nose wings to a level position. Crease wings' leading edge, and fold wingtips down along existing crease lines.

4. Add a little dihedral to the wings.

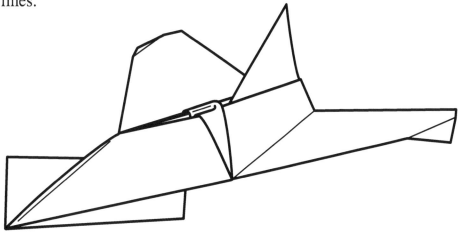

5. Completed Diamond Cruiser.

9. Speed Master

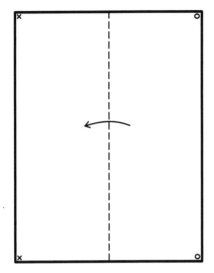

1. Fold the paper in half.

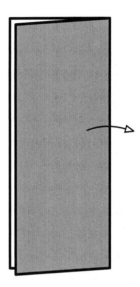

2. Unfold to its previous position.

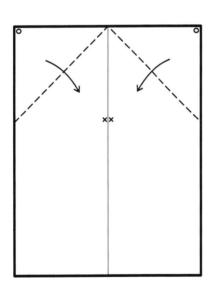

3. Fold the marked corners to the center crease line.

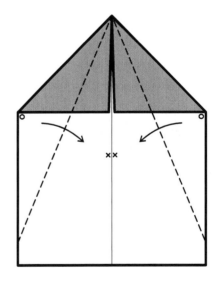

4. Fold the marked corners to the center crease line.

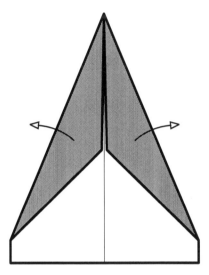

5. Unfold to step 4 position.

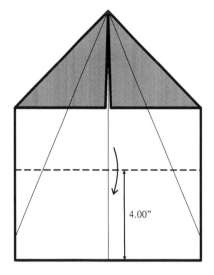

6. Fold the tip down the center crease line at 4.00" from the bottom horizontal edge.

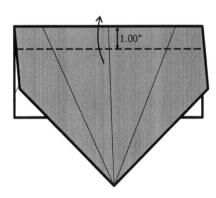

7. Fold the tip up the center crease line at 1.00" from the top horizontal edge.

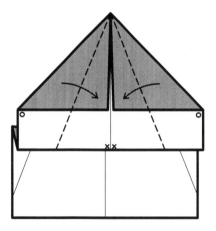

8. Fold the marked corners to the center crease line.

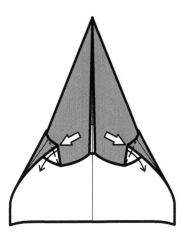

9. Hold the center part of the folds down. Push the lower portion of the two overlapping folds out, and valley fold (see "Wing Fold" on page 23).

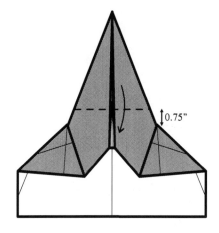

0.75"

10. Fold the tip down the center crease line at 0.75" from the wing's shoulder.

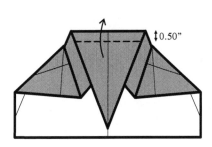

0.50"

11. Fold the tip up the center crease line at 0.50" from the top horizontal edge.

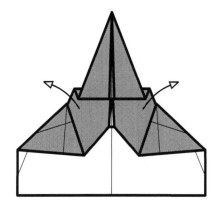

12. Unfold the model to step 13 position.

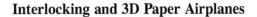

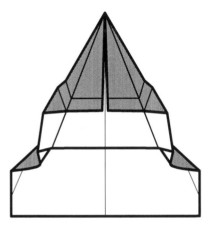

13. Model shows the unfolded position after step 12.

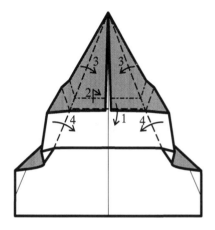

14. Inside reverse fold the top part of the model using existing crease lines created in steps 10 and 11 (see "Inside Reverse Fold" on page 19).

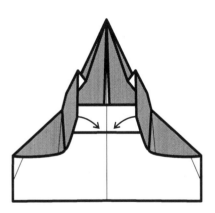

15. Model shows the intermediate stage of the fold from step 14 to step 16.

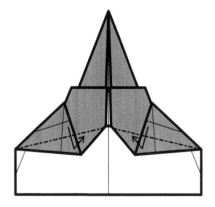

16. Fold flaps under, and insert beneath the horizontal edge created in step 7.

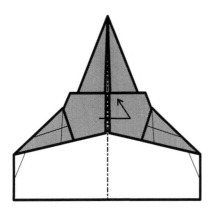

17. Mountain fold the model in half.

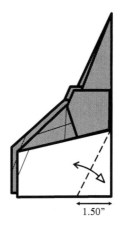

1.50"

18. Fold and unfold to make crease line for the tail fin.

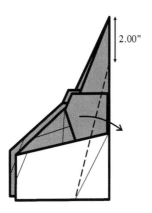

2.00"

19. Fold the top layer of the model to the right side. This fold will result in the nose twisting upward a little.

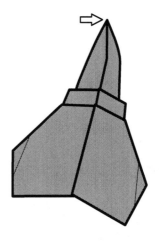

20. Gently flip the nose over to the other side. Do not let go of the model.

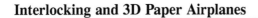

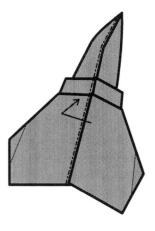

21. Mountain fold the left wing to match the right wing.

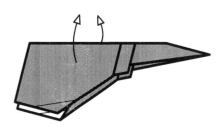

22. Unfold both wings.

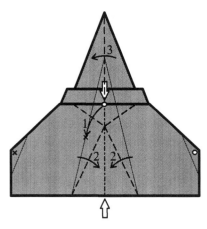

23. Lift the marked overlapping flap and the center of the bottom horizontal edge up towards you. Valley fold such that the marked point on the overlapping flap meet the crease line created in step 21 (see "Interlocking Fold" on page 27).

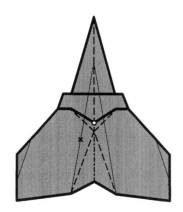

24. Model shows the intermediate stage of the fold from step 23 to step 25.

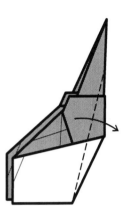

25. Fold the top layer of the wing to the right side along the existing crease line. This fold will result in the nose twisting upward a little.

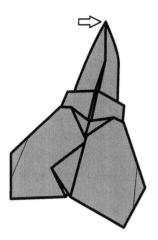

26. Gently flip the nose over to the other side.

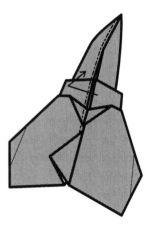

27. Mountain fold the left wing, along the existing crease line, to match the right wing.

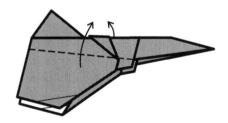

28. Fold wings up to create the fuselage.

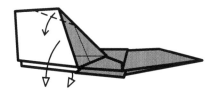

29. Unfold both wings to a level position. Crease wings' leading edge, and fold wingtips down along existing crease lines.

30. Add a little dihedral to the wings.

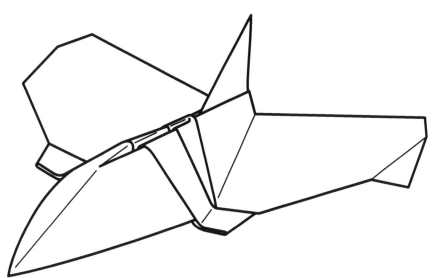

31. Completed "Speed Master".

10. Stealth Fighter

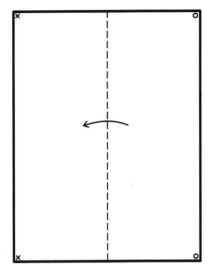

1. Fold the paper in half.

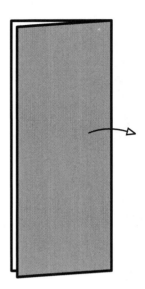

2. Unfold to its previous position.

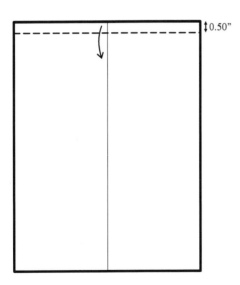

0.50"

3. Fold the top horizontal edge down the center crease line at 0.50" from the top horizontal edge.

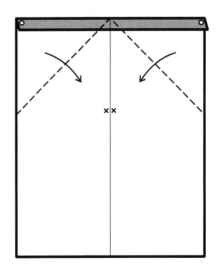

4. Fold the marked corners to the center crease line.

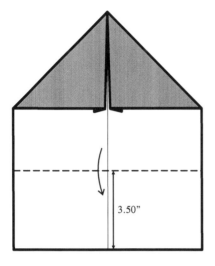

3.50"

5. Fold the tip down the center crease line at 3.50" from the bottom horizontal edge.

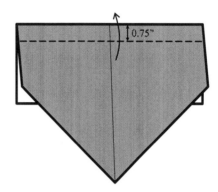

0.75"

6. Fold the tip up the center crease line at 0.75" from the top horizontal edge.

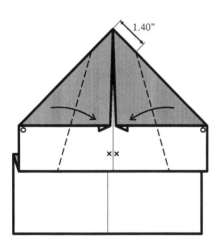

1.40"

×│×

7. Fold the marked corners to the center crease line.

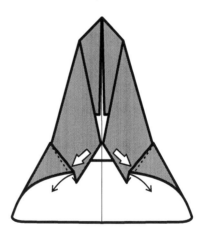

8. Hold the center part of the folds down. Push the lower portion of the two overlapping folds out, and valley fold (see "Wing Fold" on page 23).

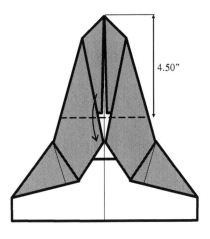

4.50"

9. Fold the tip down the center crease line at 4.50" from the tip.

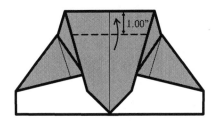

1.00"

10. Fold the tip up the center crease line at 1.00" from the top horizontal edge.

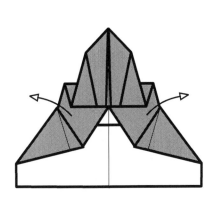

11. Unfold the model to step 7 position.

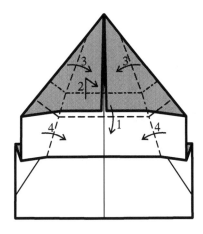

12. Inside reverse fold the top part of the model using existing crease lines created in steps 9 and 10 (see "Inside Reverser Fold" on page 19).

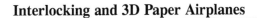

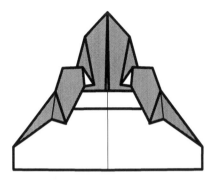

13. Model shows the intermediate stage of the fold from step 12 to step 14.

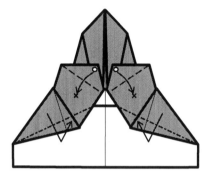

14. Fold the flaps under, and insert beneath the horizontal edge created in step 12. Fold the marked corners down to their maximum.

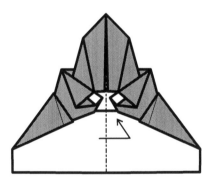

15. Mountain fold the model in half.

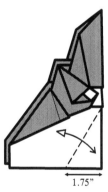

1.75"

16. Fold and unfold to create crease line for the tail fin.

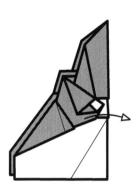

17. Unfold the model.

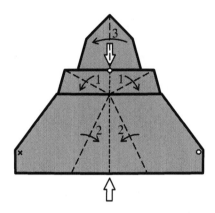

18. Lift the marked overlapping flap and the center of the bottom horizontal edge up towards you, and valley fold the model in half (see "Interlocking Fold" on page 27).

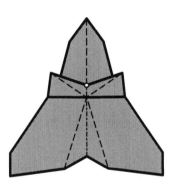

19. Model shows the intermediate stage of the fold from step 18 to step 20.

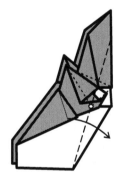

20. Fold the top layer of the model to the right side. It is important that the fold line meet the marked point on the hidden lines. This fold will result in the nose twisting upward a little.

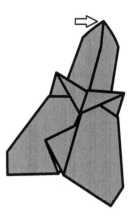

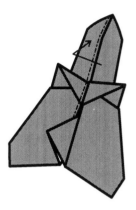

21. Gently flip the nose over to the other side.

22. Mountain fold the left wing to match the right wing.

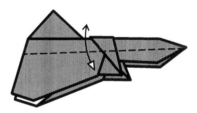

23. Fold the wings up and then down to a level position to create the fuselage.

24. Add a slight dihedral to the wings. Crease wings' leading edge.

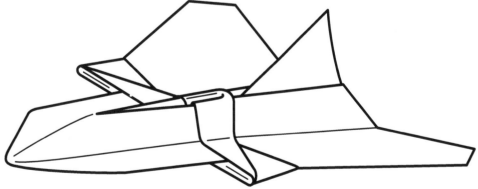

25. Completed "Stealth Fighter.

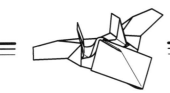

11. Typhoon

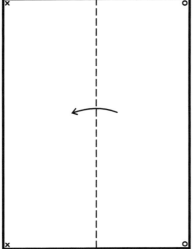

1. Fold the paper in half.

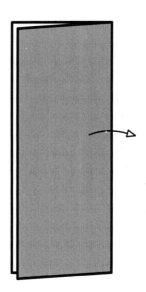

2. Unfold to its previous position.

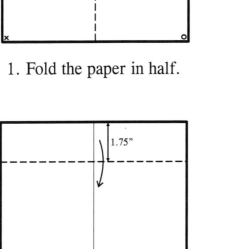

3. Fold the top horizontal edge down the center crease line at 1.75" from the top horizontal edge.

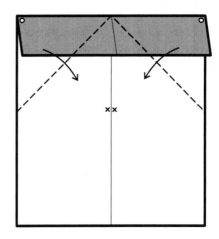

4. Fold the marked corners to the center crease line.

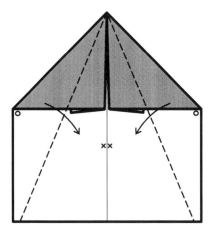

5. Fold the marked corners to the center crease line.

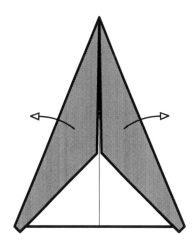

6. Unfold to step 3 position.

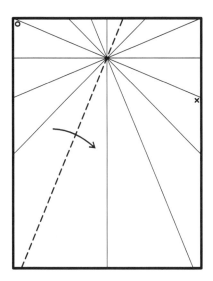

7. Fold the marked corner to the right vertical edge along the existing crease line.

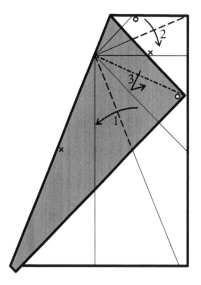

8. Fold marked points in the arrow directions along existing crease lines.

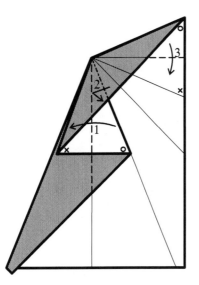

9. Fold marked corners in the arrow directions along existing crease lines.

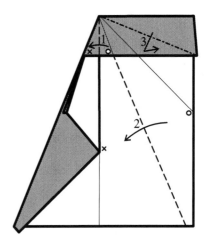

10. Fold marked points in the arrow directions along existing crease lines.

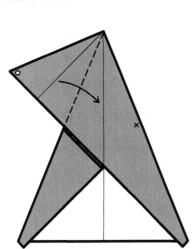

11. Fold the marked tip in the arrow direction along the existing crease line.

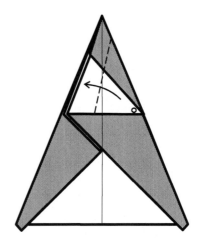

12. Fold the marked tip in the arrow direction, along a slanted fold line as shown, to create the airplane's canard.

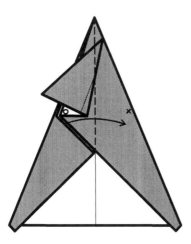

13. Fold the top three layers from the left side to the right side along the center crease line.

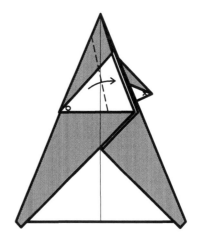

14. Fold the marked tip to the right side to match the other protruding tip.

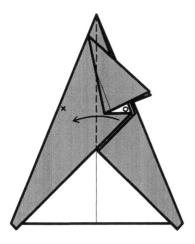

15. Fold the top two layers from the right side to the left side.

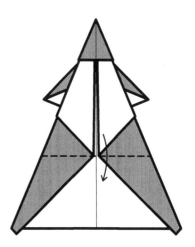

16. Fold the tip down the center crease line.

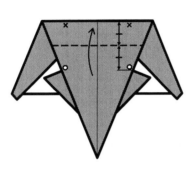

17. Fold the marked points up the center crease line to meet the top horizontal edge.

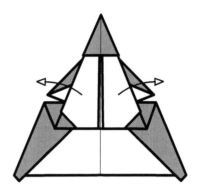

18. Unfold to step 16 position.

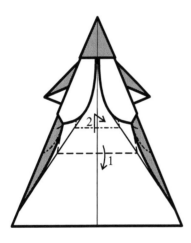

19. Inside reverse fold the model using existing crease lines created in steps 16 and 17 (see "Inside Reverse Fold" on page 19).

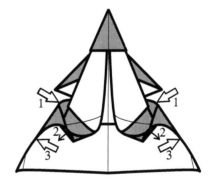

20. Push the upper part of the two side folds inward, and stretch the lower part of the two side folds outward. This is similar to creating the wing fold (see "Wing Fold" on page 23).

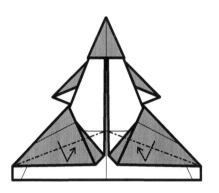

21. Fold the flaps under, and insert beneath the horizontal edge created in step 20.

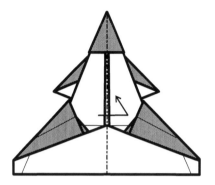

22. Mountain fold the model in half.

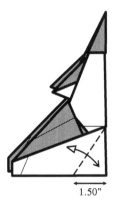

1.50"

23. Fold and unfold to create crease line for the tail fin.

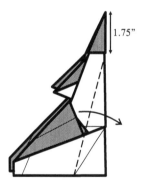

1.75"

24. Fold the top layer of the model to the right side. This fold will result in the nose twisting upward a little.

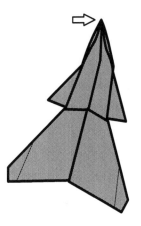

25. Gently flip the nose over to the other side. Do not let go of the model.

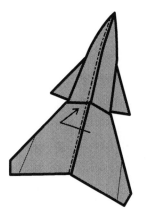

26. Mountain fold the left wing to match the right wing.

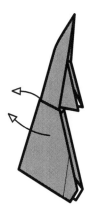

27. Unfold both wings.

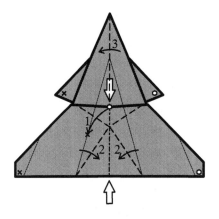

28. Lift the marked overlapping flap and the center of the bottom horizontal edge up towards you. Valley fold such that the marked point on the overlapping flap meet the crease line created in step 26 (see "Interlocking Fold" on page 27).

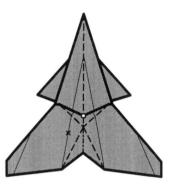

29. Model shows the intermediate stage of the fold from step 28 to step 30.

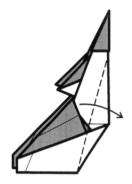

30. Fold the top layer of the wing to the right side along the existing crease line. This fold will result in the nose twisting upward a little.

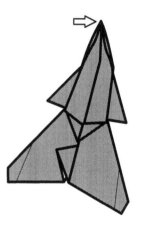

31. Gently flip the nose over to the other side.

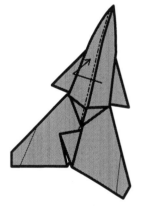

32. Mountain fold the left wing, along the existing crease line, to match the right wing.

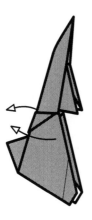

33. Unfold both wings a little.

34. Flip model over to show the bottom side.

35.   Pop open the fuselage by pulling out the marked paper edges. Holding the pulled out paper edges together with one hand, pinch down the excess paper bulge with the other hand at the location as shown by the two arrows. Crease wings' leading edge, and fold wingtips along existing crease lines.

36. Adjust the canard and wing to a level position.

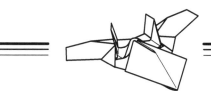

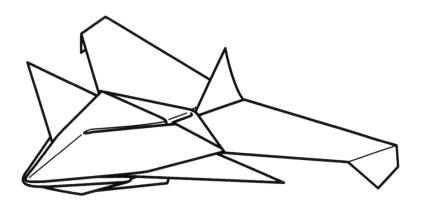

37. Top view of the completed "Typhoon".

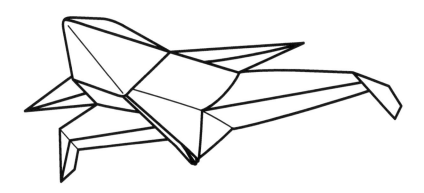

38. Bottom view of the completed "Typhoon".

12. Canard Fighter

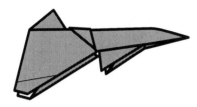

1. Make the above model by following steps 1 through 32 for the "Typhoon".

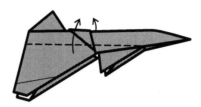

2. Fold both wings and canards up to create the fuselage.

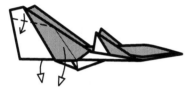

3. Unfold wings and canards to a level position. Crease wings' leading edge, and fold wingtips down along existing crease lines.

4. Adjust both wings and canards to form a slight dihedral.

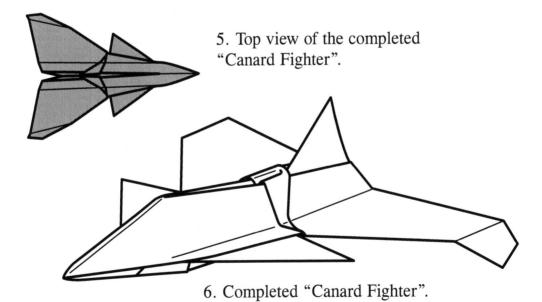

5. Top view of the completed "Canard Fighter".

6. Completed "Canard Fighter".

13. Raptor

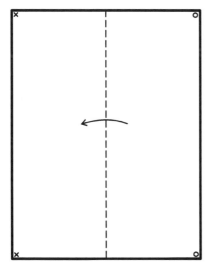

1. Fold the paper in half.

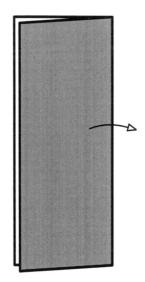

2. Unfold to its previous position.

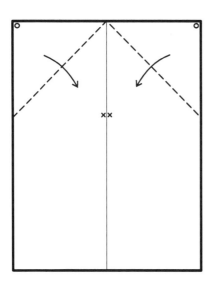

3. Fold the marked corners to the center crease line.

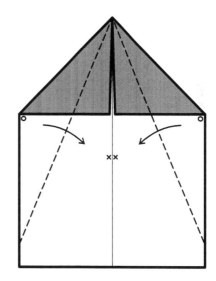

4. Fold the marked corners to the center crease line.

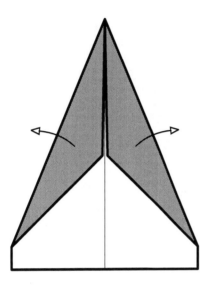

5. Unfold to step 4 position.

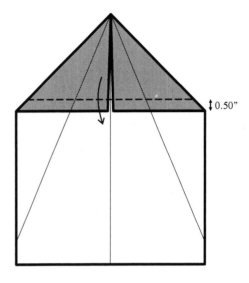

0.50"

6. Fold the tip down the center crease line at 0.50" from the horizontal edge created in step 3.

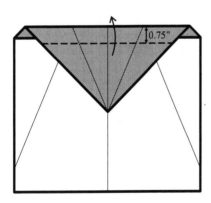

0.75"

7. Fold the tip up the center crease line at 0.75" from the top horizontal edge.

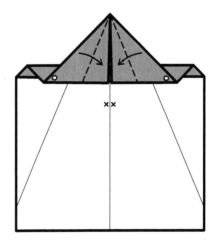

8. Fold the marked points to the center crease line.

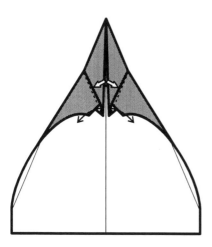

9. Hold the center part of the folds down. Push the lower portion of the two overlapping folds out, and valley fold (see "Wing Fold" on page 23).

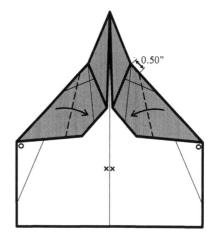

10. Fold the marked corners to the center crease line. Crease only the part shown with valley fold lines in the model above.

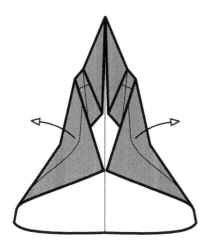

11. Unfold to step 10 position.

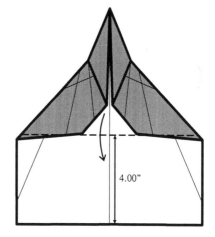

12. Fold the tip down the center crease line at 4.00" from the bottom horizontal edge.

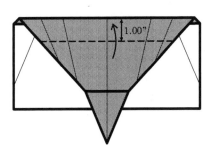

13. Fold the tip up the center crease line at 1.00" from the top horizontal edge.

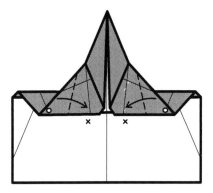

14. Fold the marked points inward along the existing crease lines created in step 10.

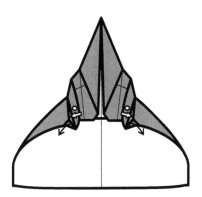

15. Hold the two marked folds down. Push the lower portion of the two overlapping folds out, and valley fold (see "Wing Fold" on page 23).

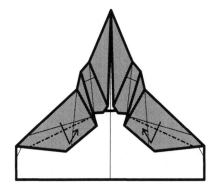

16. Fold the flaps under, and insert beneath the horizontal edge created in step 13.

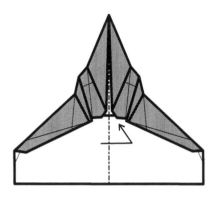

17. Mountain fold the model in half.

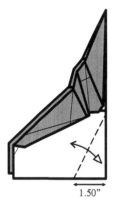

1.50"

18. Fold and unfold to create crease line for the tail fin.

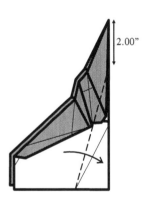

2.00"

19. Fold the top layer of the model to the right side. This fold will result in the nose twisting upward a little.

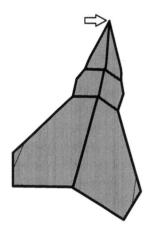

20. Gently flip the nose over to the other side. Do not let go of the model.

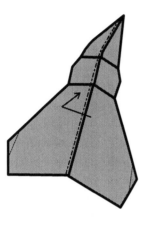

21. Mountain fold the left wing to match the right wing.

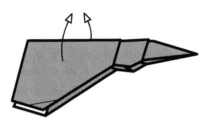

22. Unfold both wings.

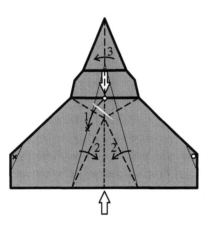

23. Lift the marked overlapping flap and the center of the bottom horizontal edge up towards you. Valley fold such that the marked point on the overlapping flap meet the crease line created in step 21 (see "Interlocking Fold" on page 27).

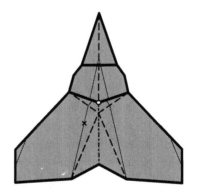

24. Model shows the intermediate stage of the fold from step 23 to step 25.

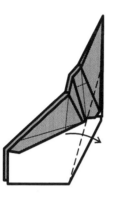

25. Fold the top layer of the wing to the right side along the existing crease line. This fold will result in the nose twisting upward a little.

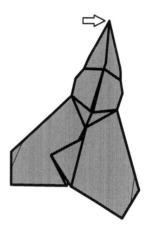

26. Gently flip the nose over to the other side.

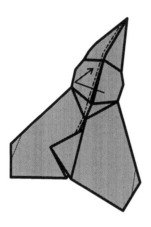

27. Mountain fold the left wing, along the existing crease line, to match the right wing.

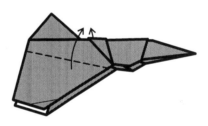

28. Fold both wings up as shown.

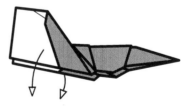

29. Unfold wings to a level position.

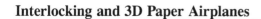

30. Flip model over to show the bottom side.

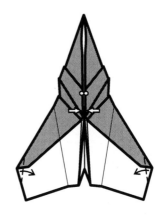

32. Model shows popped open fuselage.

31. Pop open the fuselage by pulling out the marked paper edges. Holding the pulled out paper edges together with one hand, pinch down the excess paper bulge with the other hand at the location as shown by the two arrows. Crease wings' leading edge, and fold both wingtips along the existing crease lines.

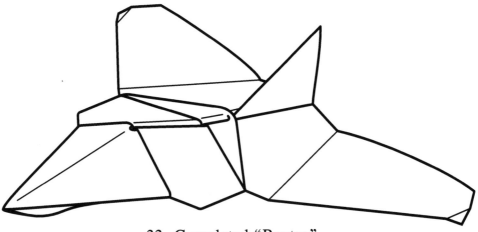

33. Completed "Raptor".

14. Tiger Shark

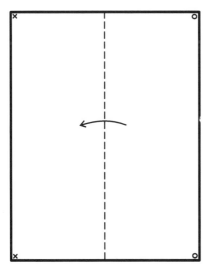

1. Fold the paper in half.

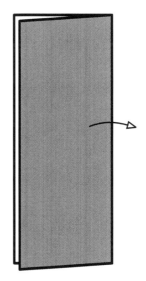

2. Unfold to its previous position.

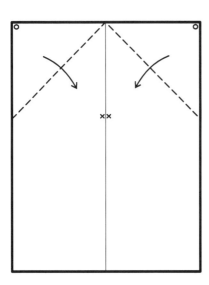

3. Fold the marked corners to the center crease line.

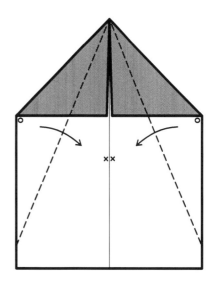

4. Fold the marked corners to the center crease line.

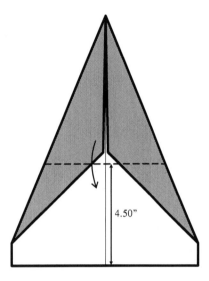

5. Fold the tip down the center crease line at 4.50" from the bottom horizontal edge.

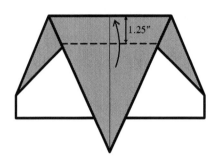

6. Fold the tip up the center crease line at 1.25" from the top horizontal edge.

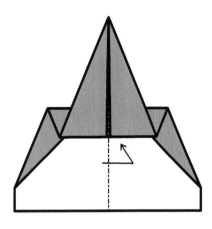

7. Mountain fold the model in half.

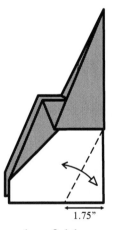

8. Fold and unfold to create crease line for the tail fin.

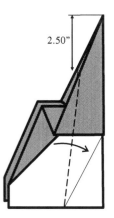

2.50"

9. Fold the top layer of the model to the right side. Repeat the same fold for the bottom layer.

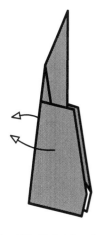

10. Unfold both wings.

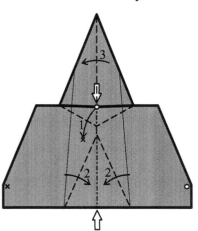

11. Lift the marked overlapping flap and the center of the bottom horizontal edge up towards you. Valley fold such that the marked point on the horizontal overlapping flap is located midway between the center crease line and the crease lines created in step 9.

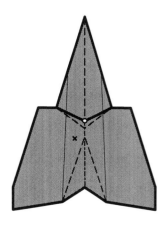

12. Model shows the intermediate stage of the fold from step 11 to step 13.

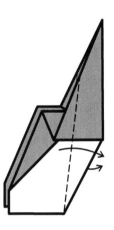

13. Fold the top layer of the model over to the right side along the existing crease line. Repeat the same fold for the bottom layer.

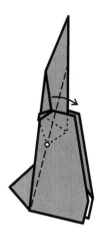

14. Fold the top layer of the fuselage over to the right side. It is important that the fold line meet the marked tip on the hidden lines. This fold will result in the nose twisting upward a little.

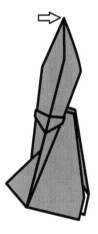

15. Gently flip the nose over to the other side.

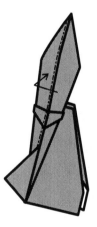

16. Mountain fold the left side of the fuselage to match the right side.

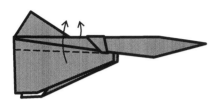

17. Fold both wings up to create the rear part of the fuselage.

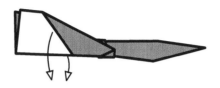

18. Unfold both wings to a level position.

19. Flip the model over to show the bottom side.

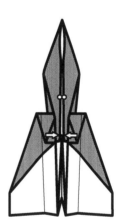

20. Pop open the fuselage by pulling out the marked paper edges. Holding the pulled out paper edges together with one hand, pinch down the excess paper bulge with the other hand at the location as shown by the two arrows. Crease wings' leading edge.

21. Model shows the popped open fuselage.

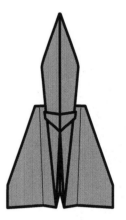

22. Top view of the completed "Tiger Shark".

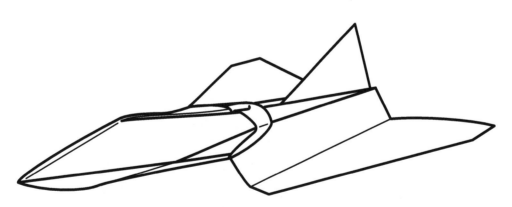

23. Completed "Tiger Shark".

15. Thunder Bird

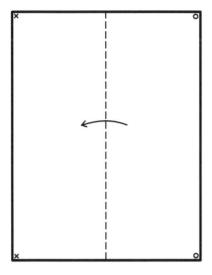

1. Fold the paper in half.

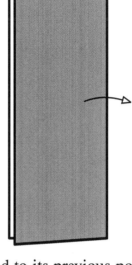

2. Unfold to its previous position.

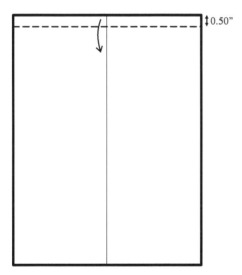

3. Fold the top horizontal edge down the center crease line at 0.50" from the top horizontal edge.

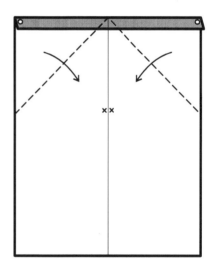

4. Fold the marked corners to the center crease line.

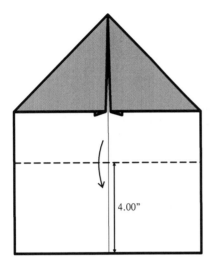

5. Fold the tip down the center crease line at 4.00" from the bottom horizontal edge.

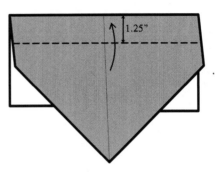

6. Fold the tip up the center crease line at 1.25" from the top horizontal edge.

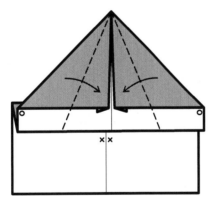

7. Fold the marked corners to the center crease line.

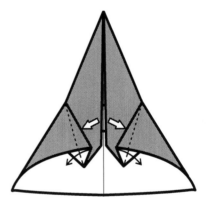

8. Hold the center part of the folds down. Push the lower portion of the two overlapping folds out, and valley fold (see "Wing Fold" on page 23).

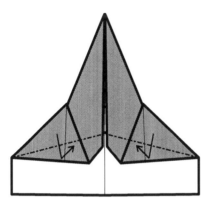

9. Fold flaps under, and insert beneath the horizontal edge created in step 6.

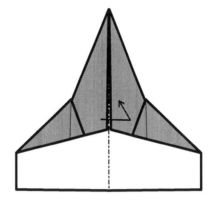

10. Mountain fold the model in half.

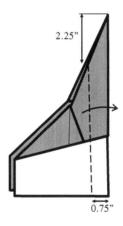

2.25"

0.75"

11. Fold the top layer of the wings to the right side.

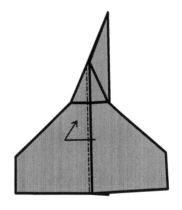

12. Mountain fold the left wing to match the right wing.

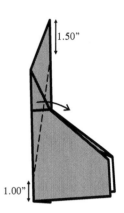

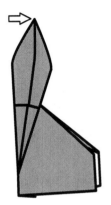

13. Fold the top layer of the upper part of the model over to the right side to create crease line for the fuselage. This fold will result in the nose twisting upward a little.

14. Gently push the nose over to the other side. Do not let go of the model.

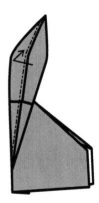

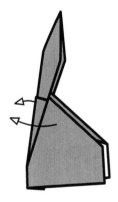

15. Mountain fold the left side of the fuselage to match the right side.

16. Unfold the model.

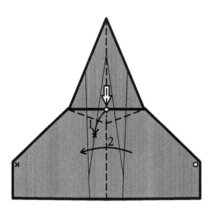

17. Lift the marked overlapping flap up towards you. Valley fold such that the marked point on the overlapping flap meet the crease line created in step 15 (see "Interlocking Fold" on page 27).

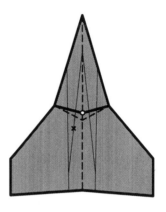

18. Model shows the intermediate stage of the fold from step 17 to step 19.

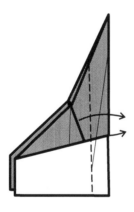

19. Fold the top layer of the model over to the right side along the existing crease line. Repeat the same fold for the bottom layer.

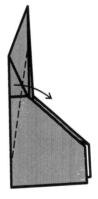

20. Fold the top layer of the upper part of the model over to the right side along the existing crease line. This fold will result in the nose twisting upward a little.

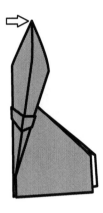

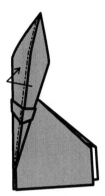

21. Gently flip the nose over to the other side.

22. Mountain fold the left side of the fuselage, along the existing crease line, to match the right side.

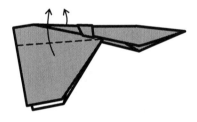

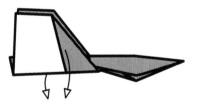

23. Fold both wings up to create the rear part of the fuselage.

24. Unfold both wings to a level position.

25. Flip model over to show the bottom side.

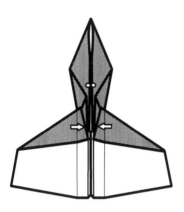

27. Model shows the popped open fuselage after step 26.

26. Pop open the fuselage by pulling out the marked paper edges. Holding the pulled out paper edges together with one hand, pinch down the excess bulge with the other hand at the location as shown by the two arrows.

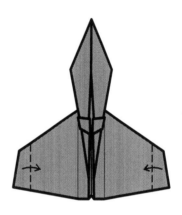

28. Crease wings' leading edge, and fold wingtips up to act as tail fins.

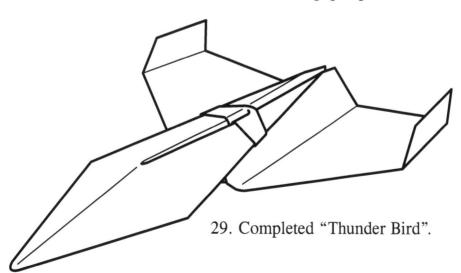

29. Completed "Thunder Bird".

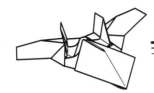

16. Twister

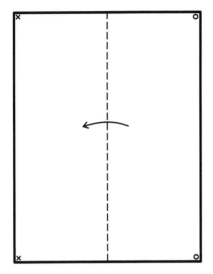

1. Fold the paper in half.

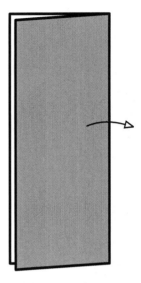

2. Unfold to its previous position.

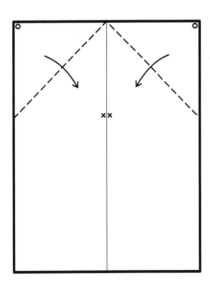

3. Fold the marked corners to the center crease line.

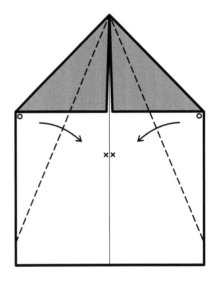

4. Fold the marked corners to the center crease line.

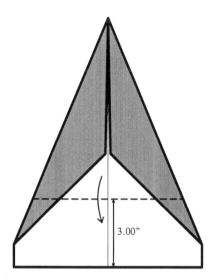

5. Fold the tip down the center crease line at 3.00" from the bottom horizontal edge.

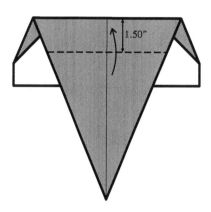

6. Fold the tip up the center crease line at 1.50" from the top horizontal edge.

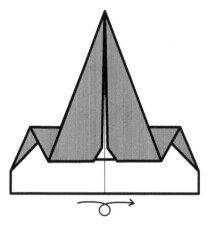

7. Flip model over.

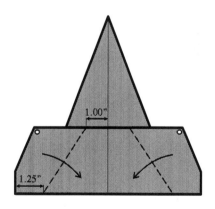

8. Fold marked corners in.

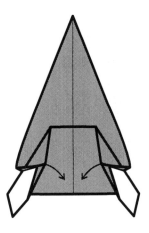

9. Model shows the intermediate stage of the fold from step 8 to step 10.

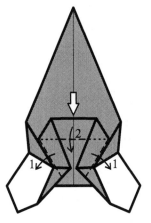

10. Fold the two side collars out, and fold the horizontal edge down the center crease line.

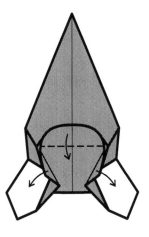

11. Model shows the intermediate stage of the fold from step 10 to step 12.

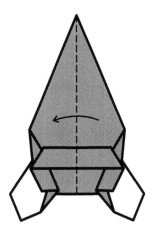

12. Valley fold the model in half.

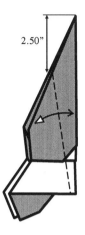

2.50"

13. Fold and unfold the top layer of the model to create crease lines. Repeat the same fold for the bottom layer.

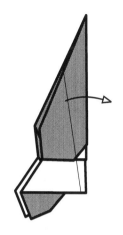

14. Unfold the model.

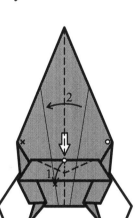

15. Lift the marked overlapping flap up towards you. Valley fold such that the marked point on the horizontal overlapping flap meet the crease lines created in step 13.

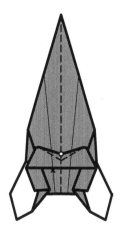

16. Model shows the intermediate stage of the fold from step 15 to step 17.

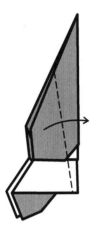

17. Fold the top layer of the wing to the right side along the existing crease line.

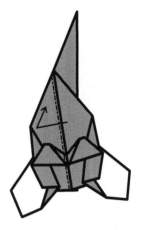

18. Mountain fold the left wing to match the right wing along the existing crease line.

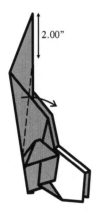

2.00"

19. Fold the top layer of the fuselage over to the right side. This fold will result in the nose twisting upward a little.

20. Gently flip the nose over to the other side.

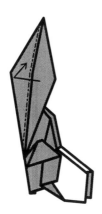

21. Mountain fold the left side of the fuselage to match the right side.

22. Fold both wings over to the left.

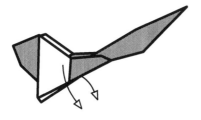

23. Unfold both wings to a level position.

24. Flip model over to show the bottom side.

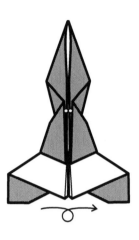

25. Pop open the fuselage by pulling out the two marked paper edges. Flip model over.

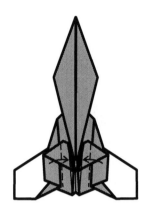

26. Fold the two tail fins up.

27. Model shows tail fins up.

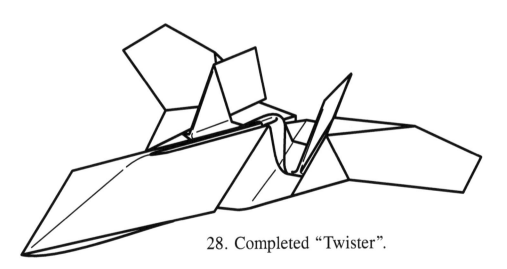

28. Completed "Twister".

Glossary

Aileron: A control surface hinged to the outer trailing edge of the wing. It can be raised or lowered for roll control.

Angle of Attack: The angle at which the chord of the wing is slanted against the airflow.

Canards: A pair of small horizontal airfoil, placed forward of an airplane's main wing, for maintaining longitudinal stability.

Center of Gravity: The point through which the resultant weight acts whatever the position the body may be in.

Chord: The line joining the leading edge to the trailing edge of a wing.

Crease: The result of a fold.

Dihedral: The upward slant of the wing, above the horizontal, that adds lateral stability.

Drag: A resistance force created when an object moves through a viscous fluid such as air or water.

Elevator: A control surface hinged to the trailing edge of the horizontal stabilizer of an airplane. It can be raised or lowered for pitch control. For paper airplane, the elevator is usually on the trailing edge of the main wing.

Fin: A vertical surface used for maintaining directional stability of an airplane.

Fuselage: The main body of the airplane.

Glide: Flying without any propulsion force other than gravitational pull.

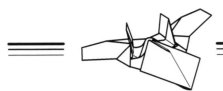

Gravity: The force that pulls object earthward.

Leading Edge: The forward edge of a wing.

Lift: The upward aerodynamic force generated by a wing moving through air.

Pitch: To nose up or down.

Roll: To rotate about the longitudinal axis, which runs from the nose to the tail of the airplane.

Rudder: A vertical control surface hinged to the trailing edge of an airplane's tail fin. It can be swung to the right or left for directional control.

Stabilizer: Fixed airfoil attached to an airplane's body for stability control.

Stall: Airflow separation, over the top surface of the wing, resulting in the total loss of lift.

Streamline: To construct so as to offer the least resistance to fluid flow.

Sweptback: The backward slant of the wing's leading edge against the airflow.

Trailing Edge: The aft edge of a wing.

Trim: To make adjustment to airplane's control surfaces.

Winglet: The bent tip of a wing that adds directional stability.

Wings: A pair of airfoil attached to the airplane to provide lift.

Yaw: To turn left or right.

ISBN 1-4120-4119-8

Made in the USA
Lexington, KY
18 January 2011